Education for a culture of peace in a gender perspective

Education for
a culture of peace
in a gender perspective

Betty A. Reardon

The Teacher's Library | **UNESCO Publishing**

The author is responsible for the choice and the presentation
of the facts contained in this book and for the opinions
expressed therein, which are not necessarily those of
UNESCO and do not commit the Organization.

Published in 2001 by the United Nations Educational,
Scientific and Cultural Organization,
7, place de Fontenoy, 75352 Paris 07 SP, France
Composed and printed by Navis imprimeur conseil, Paris 15^e
ISBN 92-3-103811-7

Printed in France

Foreword

The overall goal of this Study Unit on education for a culture of peace in a gender perspective is to assist teachers in their efforts to educate 'caring and responsible citizens, open to other cultures, able to appreciate the value of freedom, respectful of human dignity and differences, and able to prevent conflicts or resolve them by non-violent means' (Declaration and Integrated Framework of Action on Education for Peace, Human Rights and Democracy, UNESCO, 1995). As a training manual, it is primarily directed towards pre-service and in-service preparation of teachers in upper secondary schools, but may also be used at other levels of the formal school system as well as in non-formal education. We hope that the examples used by teachers and the interaction in the classroom will contribute to the broadening of the socio-cultural context, which is beyond the possibility of this manual.

UNESCO is proud to be the first to present an educational tool for the transformation towards a culture of peace that fully integrates a gender perspective. We hope that the manual will be broadly used and contribute to the development of skills and competences in non-violent and gender-responsive conflict resolution and peace building throughout the Decade for a Culture of Peace and Non-Violence for the Children of the World (2001–10) and beyond. Indeed, the strategy for the Decade includes two main aspects: first, educating for a culture of peace and second, strengthening the global movement for a culture of peace.

Like the International Year for a Culture of Peace (2000), the International Decade has as its basis the United Nations Declaration and Programme of Action on a Culture of Peace, which was adopted by the United Nations General Assembly in September 1999. Equality between women and men is one of the eight domains for action highlighted in the

Programme of Action. Consequently, we would hope that the use of this Study Unit would be an important step in the implementation of the Programme of Action. This training manual is also developed in order to help implement the Beijing Platform for Action (1995), notably Strategic Objective E.4: Promote women's contribution to fostering a culture of peace, as well as Security Council Resolution 1325 on Women, Peace and Security (2000).

The Director-General of UNESCO, Mr. Koïchiro Matsuura, has stated in the report of the conference on Higher Education for Peace, Tromsö, Norway, May 2000: 'UNESCO believes that the principal challenge facing peace education is that of ensuring justice in everyday life as a guarantee for a sufficiently broad basis for democracy. Education, both formal and informal – in schools and in the family, through mass media and social institutions – is the most important process by which we can promote the values, attitudes and behavioral patterns that are consistent with a culture of peace.'

This manual was elaborated by Dr Betty A. Reardon (Teachers College, Columbia University, New York/International Peace Research Association (IPRA)) in co-operation with the Women and a Culture of Peace Programme, Social and Human Sciences Sector and the Division for the Promotion of Quality Education, Education Sector as well as with the support of the Division for Women, Youth and Special Strategies, Bureau of Strategic Planning, UNESCO, notably through its director, Ms Breda Pavlic.

UNESCO would sincerely like to thank Dr Reardon both for her unfailing commitment to the goals of this organization and her intellectual and moral contribution to its work.

Finally, we see this manual as dynamic in the sense that it is expected to evolve and develop through a continuing dialogue with its users. We therefore encourage you to transmit to us constructive comments and feedback that will be considered for integration in future editions.

INGEBORG BREINES, Director
Women and a Culture
of Peace Programme

KAISA SAVOLAINEN, Director a.i.
Division for the Promotion of
Quality Education

Contents

PART ONE
A field in development: concepts, purposes, issues

SECTION 1
Introduction to education for a culture of peace

SECTION 2
A culture of peace: the social and personal dimensions

PART TWO
Professional and pedagogical dimensions

SECTION 6
Attributes, capacities and skills of teachers of peace

SECTION 7
Learning goals of education for a culture of peace

SECTION 8
Teaching approaches to educating for a culture of peace from a gender perspective

Note to the instructor

This resource for teacher education is constructed in two basic parts. Part One, the social foundations component, offers an overview of the developing field of education for a culture of peace, its purposes, the issues it addresses and the rationale for its development. Part Two, treating the practical, deals more specifically with the professional and methodological necessities of the field. It should be noted, however, that peace education is, in general, a field that derives from and practises holism, so that there are reflections on theory integrated into descriptions of practice throughout the text. Every component of the resource has a particular pedagogical purpose, intended to introduce the modes of inquiry and forms of thinking most conducive to learning for a culture of peace.

Each topical section of this study unit/syllabus is preceded by a box with a list of Preparatory Readings to be read as background, and some Suggested Readings follow the Learning Processes and Projects to extend and further enrich the study. The purpose of the Preparatory Readings is to offer additional substance regarding the concerns discussed in the unit. The Suggested Readings make it possible for the instructor to use this resource as a syllabus for a full course. With the exceptions of the international instruments which are essential to any study of these issues, the readings have been selected from among a wider range of possible titles. Those that appear here are for the most part in English, the language in which the unit was drafted. They are drawn from United Nations documents, the works of non-governmental organizations working in the fields of human rights, peace and gender justice, and some commercial publications. More extensive and eclectic lists are referenced in the list of Supplementary materials on page 197. While some of these titles are available in other languages, these, too, are primarily in English. Instructors, therefore, are urged to search for titles in the primary language of the students and teachers they will be guiding through this exploration of Education for a Culture of Peace in a Gender Perspective. The international instruments are available in the six official languages of the United Nations and many of them in other languages. Instructors are advised to inquire of their Foreign Ministry, Ministry of Education, their National Commission for UNESCO, United Nations Co-ordinating Offices and UNESCO Regional Office. The texts of many of these documents are also available on the Internet. The websites for these and other supplemental readings are also listed in the References. Instructors may wish to download and print them out to review in preparation for offering a unit or course.

Because we assert that all teachers must be prepared to educate for a culture of peace, this syllabus is designed to serve as one unit in a general foundation of education course. It also serves as the basis of a complete course, constructed by adding readings as suggested. The pedagogy is based on the assumption that the course will be conducted primarily in a discussion and learning activity mode, reflecting the interactive, participatory pedagogy advocated in peace education. It suggests that a portion of the class time be devoted to demonstration teaching to enable class participants to have practical experience of some of the proposed learning processes through which they will be able, in turn, to lead their own students. We recognize that such exercises are more commonly found in courses on methods rather than those in the philosophical or substantive bases of education. However, because of the importance of the participatory element of peace education and the wide advocacy in the field of the integration of theory and practice, practical possibilities for teaching at various levels of schooling are included. It is suggested that the preparatory readings and preparation of the learning exercises be completed before the sessions in which they are addressed. The Learning

Processes are based on several of the most important techniques that peace education uses to develop some of the human capacities described here as essential to achieve and enjoy a culture of peace in a world of social justice and gender equality. The Learning Processes are as integral to this text as a reflective participatory pedagogy is to peace education.

This book is offered as a prototype rather than a definitive text. It is intended to be suggestive of a range of possibilities teacher educators can adapt to their own cultures, particular students and teaching circumstances. Instructors are encouraged to develop their own discussion questions and learning activities, and to make adjustments and amendments that would better suit the material to the needs of their students, keeping in mind that the core purposes of mainstreaming peace and gender perspectives in education must remain the focus of the course of study. Many assertions about education, gender and peace are made throughout the unit. Instructors should encourage students to critically examine these assertions, interpret them within their own cultural contexts, even to challenge them. The cultivation of critical thinking is a central purpose of the pedagogy described in this prototype syllabus.

Every participant in the course should have a personal copy of this text as the core reading and, if possible, copies of the texts of the relevant United Nations documents. All are available at a minimal cost from the United Nations regional offices and/or from the World Wide Web.

PART ONE

A field in development: concepts, purposes, issues

Section 1

Introduction to education
for a culture of peace

• The purposes of this study unit

Education for a culture of peace is the most recent development in
the field of peace education which has been a main area of
UNESCO's work since its founding. This development is welcomed
by those who have advocated a comprehensive and holistic
approach to peace education. It provides an overarching concept
under which the many and varied topics and approaches that
comprise the field can be integrated, and more easily
comprehended as multiple components of a single field of
education. The concept of a culture of peace is also a clarifying

1. The numbers in square brackets refer to the Supplementary materials on p. 195.

agent that enables us to grasp more fully the social purposes of peace education. When we combine that clarifying concept with the concept of gender we are also able to understand in truly human terms the nature of the core problems that peace education is designed to address. Some of these problems are introduced in Section 5.

The achievement of any social goal requires education. Members of any community who are determined to bring about new social conditions have long realized that the community must come to understand the nature of the proposed changed conditions, the need for the changes and what will be involved in achieving them. When the United Nations General Assembly proclaimed the International Decade for a Culture of Peace and Nonviolence for the Children of the World (see reference 4), the goals of the Decade (2000–2010), as stated in the United Nations Declaration and Programme of Action on a Culture of Peace, were affirmed by millions around the world determined to bring into being a global culture of peace. Embracing such goals acknowledges that the world community must educate for a culture of peace. This syllabus is intended to serve as a tool to facilitate such education. In accordance with the Programme of Action, it is also designed to integrate gender into peace studies and peace education, an essential but lamentably neglected element of the field [4].

The emergence of a movement for a culture of peace, catalysed by UNESCO's Culture of Peace Project, is evident in many global campaigns and initiatives. The process is unfolding simultaneously with the first attempts of the United Nations to 'mainstream gender', manifest in different ways in various parts of the world, under ever-changing, widely diverse conditions and in many different cultural contexts. This syllabus is designed also as general framework for adaptation to these various circumstances and multiple cultures. Peace education is fundamental and essential to this process.

Education, whether it takes place in the family, places of worship, community organizations, the workplace or the school, is a primary medium through which culture is systematically transmitted and social goals are clarified. A culture of peace can only be achieved if those who guide the institutions and processes of education intentionally undertake to educate for peace. This study unit is one tool to enable them to do so by preparing classroom teachers to teach for peace education from a gender perspective. Properly prepared teachers would be able to guide learners through an inquiry into what would comprise a culture of peace, why such a culture is essential to the survival of human civilization and what changes in attitudes, values, behaviours and institutions will be required to achieve such a culture.

While people are educated in many different spheres of life and receive much of their lifelong education through the media or social interactions, the official, formal education provided by schools is the form in which socialization to the political culture of the community is most intentionally and systematically pursued. Schools are the institutions most essential to education for a culture of peace. Teachers are the most responsible, influential and significant agents in the schooling process. This study unit, while adaptable to other areas of learning, is designed to educate teachers of upper elementary and secondary schools, and most especially for those preparing to perform as responsible professionals.

• The rationale for education for a culture of peace from a gender perspective

When UNESCO undertook the task of promoting the concept and goal of a culture of peace, it affirmed the aspirations of human society for a life in peace that had been trapped in a culture of war and violence. More significantly, it proclaimed that these aspirations were achievable. The organization has set about the task of identifying the possibilities for change towards a culture of peace and of finding within the areas of its competence those avenues most likely to lead to the fulfilment of those possibilities. Education is one of those avenues along which most members of the human family can make their way into the realization of the vision of a positive global future put forth by the concept of a culture of peace. The United Nations Decade for a Culture of Peace and Non-violence for the Children of the World is a mobilizing force for efforts to bring about some of the significant changes in global politics and institutions intended 'to avoid the scourge of war'. Multiple movements have been formed, campaigns launched and world conferences held to lead us to one or another of these changes. These movements have resulted in multiple agreements on arms control, a potentially transformative set of international norms and standards on gender equality and universal human rights, and innumerable projects for development and poverty reduction, protection of the environment, raising world health and literacy standards. Many positive global changes have been achieved.

But wars persist among and within nations. Societies are severely plagued by various forms of political, economic, social, cultural, ecological and gender violence. Together these forms of violence form a global culture of which the 'war system' is the structural core. This system of vast military forces, ever-expanding supplies of weaponry, and constant readiness for combat is maintained by political and economic institutions and social attitudes that deem such a system necessary to national and international security. It perpetuates the use of violence for political and economic purposes, infecting our societies and distorting our cultures.

War also reinforces and exploits gender stereotypes and exacerbates, even encourages, violence against women. Changing these circumstances, devising a peace system, and bringing forth a culture of peace requires an authentic partnership between men and women. Such a system would take fully into account the potential and actual roles of women in public policy and peace-making as advocated in UNESCO's Statement on Women's Contribution to a Culture of Peace [5]. Such participation would indicate an authentic partnership, based on the equality of the partners. Equality between men and women is an essential condition of a culture of peace. Thus education for gender equality is an essential component of education for a culture of peace.

UNESCO was the first international organization to give voice to a deeper and more comprehensive understanding of the profundity and breadth of the changes required to liberate human society from the war trap and its sexist practices. The concept of a culture of peace helps to illuminate the conditions and causes of most forms of violence, to reveal the roots of war, to go deeper than conflictual relationships, national, political or ideological rivalries, even deeper than the institutions and policies that maintain the war system of national militaries, arms races and imbalanced economic priorities. The culture of violence is the aggregation of world views, ways of thinking and problem-solving that lead to the continuous use of violence and armed force. It permeates social attitudes, individual and group behaviours, and human relations from the most intimate and fundamental to the most distant and institutional. In a culture of war and violence, human inequality is assumed to be natural and violence in the pursuit of social and political purposes is legitimized as necessary and inevitable. Gender roles are cast in the mould of these assumptions and beliefs. Ideologies of 'gender apartheid' are deeply embedded in the war system and the culture of violence. The quest for a culture of peace calls on us to examine the ways in which gender roles and all forms of human inequality are woven into the fabric of cultures of violence.

Some peace educators have argued that the failure of many of the United Nations' advances noted above to lead to a more stable and lasting peace was due in large part to the lack of education for peace, as well as a lack of a comprehensive vision and a comprehensible definition of peace. This argument is well summarized in the motto of the University for Peace, *Si vis pacem parem pacem*. If we truly wish peace, we would prepare for it by educating all of our peoples about what peace is, the obstacles that impede it, the proposed and possible means to achieve it, what we need to learn to pursue these means to successful conclusions and, most important of all, the changes we must bring about in ourselves, our societies and our cultures. This unit seeks to add gender to that list of learning goals. Much of what comprises this educational task is outlined in UNESCO's Declaration and Integrated Framework of Action on Education for Peace, Human Rights and Democracy. When the General Conference of UNESCO in 1994 declared the need for such education, endorsing the Declaration of the Ministers of Education, the educational establishments of the Member States acknowledged public responsibility to deliver such education.

> We, the Ministers of Education meeting at the 44th session of the International Conference on Education,
>
> *Deeply concerned* by the manifestations of violence, racism, xenophobia, aggressive nationalism and violations of human rights, by religious intolerance, by the upsurge of terrorism in all its forms and manifestations and by the growing gap separating wealthy countries from poor countries, phenomena which threaten the consolidation of peace and democracy both nationally and internationally and which are all obstacles to development,
>
> *Mindful* of our responsibility for the education of citizens committed to the promotion of peace, human rights and democracy in accordance with the letter and spirit of the Charter of the United Nations, the Constitution of UNESCO, the Universal Declaration of Human Rights and other relevant instruments such as the Convention on the Rights of the Child and the convention on the rights of women, and in accordance with the Recommendation concerning Education for International Understanding, Co-operation and Peace and Education relating to Human Rights and Fundamental Freedoms.

The need and urgency of realizing the goals and objectives articulated in the Framework were also pronounced by 10,000 world citizens in *The Hague Agenda for the 21st Century*, adopted in the final session of The Hague Appeal for Peace Civil Society Conference held in the Netherlands in May 1999. The participants in the Conference launched a number of campaigns towards the abolition of war and the achievement of a culture of peace. Among them was the Global Campaign for Peace Education. The initial statement of the Global Campaign for Peace Education is a very brief but comprehensive articulation of a rationale for undertaking universal education for a culture of peace:

> A culture of peace will be achieved when citizens of the world understand global problems; have the skills to resolve conflict constructively; know and live by international standards of human rights, gender and racial equality; appreciate cultural diversity; and respect the integrity of the Earth. Such learning cannot be achieved without intentional, sustained and systematic education for peace. The urgency and necessity of such education was acknowledged by the Member States of UNESCO in 1974 and reaffirmed in the Integrated Framework of Action on Education for Peace, Human Rights, and Democracy in 1994. Yet, few educational institutions have undertaken such action. It is time to call upon ministries of education, educational institutions and policy-makers to fulfill the commitments. A campaign to facilitate the introduction of peace and human rights education into all educational institutions was called for by The Hague Appeal for Peace Civil Society Conference in May 1999. An initiative of individual educators and education NGOs committed to peace, it is conducted through a global network of education associations, and regional, national and local task forces of citizens and educators who will lobby and inform ministries of education and teacher-education institutions about the UNESCO Framework and the multiplicities of methods and materials that now exist to practice peace education in all learning environments. The goal of the campaign is to assure that all educational systems throughout the world will educate for a culture of peace [The Hague Appeal for Peace Global Campaign for Peace Education, May 1999].

Introduction to education for a culture of peace

• The conceptual framework of the study unit

While the task of achieving a culture of peace is complex and multifaceted, it is conceived in a vision of planetary wholeness. A culture of peace would be the human analogue of a healthy ecosystem composed of complementary, functionally integrated forms of biodiversity. It would bring together in a mutually enhancing way all of the world's human cultures, each maintaining its own integrity while functioning in a complementary fashion with all others to achieve a global society sustained in peace through the acknowledgement and pursuit of common human values. The framework of this syllabus is holistically constructed around a core of the common human values articulated in the international human-rights standards. The values are explored through a set of global problems embedded in the culture of war and violence as viewed through the lens of gender. Study of the problems is directed at learning goals defined as human and personal capacities. The educational approach is essentially conceptual, based on the belief that education should be a process of presenting ideas and ways of thinking relevant to the social purposes that are the foundation of any citizen education programme. The ideas and ways of thinking most relevant to the purposes advocated here derive from the concepts of culture, peace and gender. All of the various concepts discussed in each session of this study unit are tools for exploring ideas and ways of thinking that will deepen understanding of these concepts and how to work with them so as to bring about a culture of peace. Such concepts are highlighted at the end of each section as the foundations of its content.

The portions of the syllabus dealing with human capacities, social skills and learning goals are inspired by the four pillars of education, the areas of learning outlined in the report to UNESCO of the International Commission on Education for the Twenty-first Century [6]. These pillars: learning to know, to do, to be and to live together appear as strands woven throughout the unit.

The study unit/syllabus also derives from the imperatives and approaches of the Declaration and Integrated Framework of Action on Education for Peace, Human Rights and Democracy. The Framework seeks to assert the interrelationships among the various forms of international education that have been developed since the founding of UNESCO, and to approach them as one common field. In the same spirit, this syllabus seeks to encourage an integrated view of the problems that pose the major obstacles to a culture of peace, viewing them as characteristics of the 'war system' that forms the political core of the culture of war and violence. It also seeks to integrate the learning objectives into a general strategy for change towards a culture of peace, and to relate them to the resolution of the particular global problems and the characteristics of a culture of peace.

Because teachers are the most significant of all learners in the process of developing an education adequate to the tasks enjoined in the Integrated Framework, the document is used here as a foundation and a directional impetus for teacher education, and supplies references for more detailed and specific study. It should be carefully reviewed by all who are preparing to educate for a culture of peace.

• Core values and ethical principles as curriculum foundations

The Integrated Framework, one of the inspirations for the holistic approach of the unit, which asserts an interrelationship among the various forms of international and peace education, is primarily a normative document. Educators would place it among those other documents outlining the fundamental standards that the world community considers as essential to a just and peaceful society. The Framework also serves as a curriculum outline in that it summarises the issues and problems that should constitute the content of education for a culture of peace and states a set of objectives that are derived from fundamental human values. As such it has a place among the various normative and ethical instruments through which the United Nations has worked to create the global conditions necessary to the fulfilment of its obligations to guide the world community to the status aspired to in Article 28 of the Universal Declaration of Human Rights: 'Everyone is entitled to a social and international order in which the rights and freedoms set forth in this Declaration can be fully realized.'

The Universal Declaration of Human Rights is the heart of this evolving normative system. The rights it declares are an inventory of the values which can guide us to a Culture of Peace. Were we to describe a vision of peace in terms of the way of life it would provide the human family, we might elaborate a description of a society in which these rights are indeed, normal, the fully accepted conditions that all societies actively and constantly seek to realize. The thirty articles comprise a diagnosis of the ills of the world which cause direct and specific human suffering, an inventory of most of the forms of the global epidemic of violence which must be cured to achieve a healthy, viable culture of peace. The Declaration, all the human rights conventions and covenants, and the declarations, agendas and plans of action of the various world conferences called to address particular problems that have been identified since the promulgation of the United Nations Charter and the Declaration form a general prescription for treatment of these problems as the first step towards transformation from a culture of violence to a culture of peace.

We can consider the body of normative instruments which comprise international human rights law to be a fundamental system of global ethics, the normative seeds that properly tended will germinate a culture of peace. The central philosophical principles of the system are the complementary concepts of non-violence and humanity. These ethical, normative principles and the universal standards of human rights should thus be the foundations of all education for a culture of peace and teachers of all subjects should, as is asserted in the Integrated Framework, have a basic familiarity with them.

Among the international efforts to develop a system of norms and ethics for the international community, gender is a somewhat late arrival. It arrived with the entry of the worldwide women's movement into the development and human rights discourses. The United Nations had acknowledged the issue of the unequal status of women from its earliest days. A Commission on the Status of Women was established among the earliest of United Nations bodies. First concerns were with legal and political equality. In 1954 a Convention on the Political Rights of Women came into force, stating women's right to vote and hold elected office. From the first United Nations World Conference on Women in 1975, the focus came to be on women's role in development and problems of economic discrimination and exclusion. To the present day these issues are of concern and their amelioration forms the major goals of the Convention on the Elimination of All Forms of Discrimination against Women (1980). Over the last decades of the twentieth century the focus was on the human rights of women, all forms of violence against women, and women's roles in armed conflict and peace-making. It has been recognized that not only war, but virtually all institutions and policies have different effects on men and women, and that understanding those differences is vital to proposing and implementing effective United Nations policies and programmes. Gender mainstreaming is intended to serve this purpose. Thus, gender is a perspective essential both to the envisioning and development of a culture of peace and to the education necessary to achieve it.

Gender pervades every aspect of our lives, forming one of the most significant factors in social, economic, political and cultural affairs. It should affect how we view all of the major global problems. It has a great and largely unrecognized effect on the nature and the outcomes of the policies proposed to resolve them. In spite of its fundamental importance, gender as a concept and as a determining element in human society is not generally understood, nor is it adequately considered in policy making. Yet when we consider the main normative concepts and social values integral to a culture of peace, gender may be one of the most essential. This unit will attempt to shed some light on gender as a factor in resolving the problems of violence and creating the conditions of peace, so that teachers can educate in a manner that gives to gender the significance it warrants.

• Mainstreaming gender and peace: the social purposes and the learning goals of education for a culture of peace

The 'mainstreaming' of a gender perspective as declared by the United Nations is the policy through which the organization intends to remedy the inequities and problems arising from failure to respond adequately to gender bias and lack of gender perspective in the formation of all United Nations policy. United Nations policy reflects and derives from the positions of the Member States. So, it appears that similar inequities and problems exist in most Member States. Gender mainstreaming, then, is a policy that could serve the cause of human dignity and social equality in most societies. If gender consequences are to become a constant and common factor in policy-making, policy-makers and ordinary citizens must be educated to understand gender and how it has such significant and pervasive effects upon most aspects of our personal and social lives and how it impacts on politics, economics, environment and the fulfilment of human-rights standards.

The Declaration of the Ministers of Education participating in the forty-fourth session of the International Conference on Education can be interpreted as a call to mainstream education for a culture of peace while confronting gender bias. It states that because

> education policies have to contribute to the development of understanding, solidarity and tolerance among individuals and among ethnic, social, cultural and religious groups and sovereign nations, . . . education should promote knowledge, values, attitudes and skills conducive to respect for human rights and to an active commitment to the defence of such rights and to the building of a culture of peace and democracy,

[We shall] *Strive resolutely:*

> 2.1 to base education on principles and methods that contribute to the development of the personality of pupils, students and adults who are respectful of their fellow human beings and determined to promote peace, human rights and democracy;

> 2.2 to take suitable steps to establish in educational institutions an atmosphere contributing to the success of education for international understanding, so that they become ideal places for the exercise of tolerance, respect for human rights, the practice of democracy and learning about the diversity and wealth of cultural identities;

> 2.3 to take action to eliminate all direct and indirect discrimination against girls and women in education systems and to take specific measures to ensure that they achieve their full potential. . . .

As follows from the ethical character of a culture of peace and the changes in values and perceptions that are necessary to achieve it, the main learning goals to be pursued are normative and conceptual. We seek to engender an understanding of the conceptual tools that can be applied to critical and creative thinking about issues of peace, human rights and democracy as we endeavour to help teachers to understand, espouse and communicate the core values we hold to be the essence of a culture of peace. The achievement of these values, each of which informs one of the human capacities designated as the overarching learning goals, is the fundamental social purpose of education for a culture of peace. All education has fundamental social purposes. Education is planned to achieve the common purposes of the educating society. Those who advocate striving for a culture of peace argue that the global society should be guided by core values that would benefit this planet and all humankind. Some of these values – environmental sustainability, cultural diversity, human solidarity, social responsibility and gender equality – are defined in Section 8 with the human capacities through which they might be realized.

The related human capacities specified as the learning goals of this syllabus are: (a) ecological awareness; (b) cultural competency; (c) global agency; (d) conflict proficiency; and (e) gender sensitivity. The development of these capacities could give rise to a change in perceptions that could, in turn, initiate the change in human consciousness that many argue is the first and most fundamental base from which, as noted in the Preamble to the Constitution of UNESCO, 'peace must be constructed'. Teaching methods for the development of these general capacities will be presented where they are most relevant throughout the syllabus.

• Thinking about culture, peace and gender

The process of mainstreaming in education as in policy-making involves thinking not only conceptually about what is to be mainstreamed, but also strategically about how to do it.

If culture, peace and gender are to be mainstreamed into education, then educators must think about those concepts in terms that lend themselves to learning. Learning is above all about the evolution of changes in individuals, comprising the development of their capacities, the refinement of skills, the acquisition of knowledge, the cultivation of values and assuming a place in the world. Learning is a dynamic and continuous process that occurs throughout the lives of individuals and the histories of peoples and nations. Advances in the human condition are the product of human learning. Accordingly, educators are encouraged to consider the pursuit of the core value and problem concepts of this syllabus as dynamic humanly guided processes, not as fixed conditions of human societies. All of these concepts are intended to be tools for teachers who undertake to educate for a culture of peace to use in preparing learners to participate in the process.

Culture is the sum total of a people's way of life, their world views, their spiritual and religious beliefs, history and collective memory, arts, language and literature, social institutions, social and personal relations. Culture is the way in which we realize our humanity, our human commonalties and human differences. Virtually every aspect of our lives is influenced by the cultures in which they are lived. Because culture profoundly influences human identity and behaviour, it is the source from which the concepts and qualities of gender and peace flow into human consciousness.

War is an institution that has evolved in virtually all human cultures. In some cultures it has been the main organizing institution, determining economic practices, forms of education and social class as well as gender roles. Class is reflected in military hierarchies with the privileged classes holding command positions and the deprived making up the ranks of the combat troops who suffer greater casualties. War has been one of the main determinates of gender difference and the social value accorded each sex. Men plan and wage war. Women provide the basic life-supporting services for the society, reproduce and serve the warriors, care for the wounded, mourn the dead and the defeats of their nations and pass on to their children the stories of their people's experience of war, whether considered glorious or ignoble.

The institution of war is nourished and maintained by a culture of war and violence. The artefacts of this culture are found in monuments, celebrated in holidays, art, films and literature depicting war as glorious and heroic, martial music marking public ceremonies and important social occasions, children's war games and computer games, violent competitive sports, even, some would say, competitive school examinations. A number of educators believe that the competitive ethos that prevails in many classrooms around the world is one indicator of how the culture of war has affected education. Others claim that the competitive classroom is a necessary preparation for life. We are so immersed in these cultures that we do not fully perceive them.

In the complex world of today the ever present and pervasive organization for war is not so readily visible, nor are the patriarchal foundations of war. Women now serve in the military, a few of them reaching high rank in the centres of power. However, they are still only a small minority of those who determine issues of war and peace and policy-making for peace and security. In military matters, as in other public affairs, the changes occurring in gender relations and gender roles have had little impact. War and security issues still remain in most cultures and societies the domain of men from which women are excluded. There is, however, a growing recognition of the severe, negative impact of war and militarized security on women. United Nations Security Council Resolution 1325 (2000) on women, peace and security, a historic resolution that deserves full attention in regards to its implementation, acknowledges women's important role in conflict prevention and resolution.

At the beginning of the twentieth century, the casualties of war were predominantly men killed and wounded on the battlefield. At the end of the century when war was waged against civil populations and social infrastructures, women and children formed the majority of those who became casualties of armed conflict more within than between nations. Cultures of war and violence and severe gender inequality are evident throughout the world. Many now believe that gender injustice and war are so integral one to the other that a culture of peace depends as much on the achievement of gender justice and equality between women and men as it does on disarmament and demilitarization.

Peace is a set of conditions in which diverse peoples share their common planet, cultivating mutually enhancing relationships, respecting the dignity and rights of all, appreciating the richness of their diversity while living in harmony with the natural environment. World peace would mean an end to the institution of war and the beginning of new, positive possibilities for the human family. It would provide the conditions in which all the other forms of violence manifested in the culture of violence could also be overcome. It would see the international standards on human rights become the basic operating rules of most societies, assuring respect for the dignity, integrity and identity of all persons and peoples. Life would be sustained by a biologically diverse and healthy natural, planetary environment. People could expect that their fundamental physical and primary psychological and social needs would be met. Communities would be protected from avoidable harm and conflicts would be resolved without violence. In sum, world peace would mean the realization of comprehensive and authentic human security. The United Nations has described the purpose of striving towards a Culture of Peace, as 'the transformation of violent competition into co-operation based on the sharing of values and goals' (UN DOC. A/53/370, October 1998, Article 2, p. 7).

The ways in which peace is achieved and maintained change with time and circumstance. Peace is not a fixed goal. It is the changeable, positive social and political circumstances in which goals can be pursued and differences resolved without harm to others or the environment. It has been said that 'peace is a process, a way of solving problems' and that 'there is no way to peace. Peace is the way.' Such sayings instruct us in the dynamic nature of the kind of peace that would provide the foundation for a culture of peace.

Gender too is a dynamic and changeable concept. Gender roles and definitions are socially constructed and culturally conditioned ideas that determine what it means to be a woman or a man. Just as the war system and the culture of violence are far more than the institution of war, gender is more than sex, the biological differences between men and women and the social roles they perform. Biological difference is an innate physical characteristic. While this is true, it is also important to understand that even these differences of 'secondary sexual characteristics' are on a continuum. Physical characteristics among women vary greatly as they do among men. Some males manifest physical characteristics associated with females and vice versa. The significant differences between the two sexes are those of the respective reproductive systems of male and female. The gender differences we think of as feminine and masculine are determined by culture and assigned value by society. Concepts of masculinity and femininity vary among cultures and societies as do ideas about appropriate roles and behaviours for men and women. In some societies, gender roles have changed very little over long periods of time, coming to be seen as immutable or derived from nature. In others the changes have followed a more rapid rate of social and economic change, so that gender roles are more fluid and less rigid. None the less, throughout the world, gender continues to be a factor that limits choices and possibilities for both men and women. How gender roles affect each sex and how each is differently affected by social conditions, public policies and global problems are fundamental to any inquiry into learning to achieve the gender justice and human equality integral to the establishment of a culture of peace.

As we inquire into the possibilities of educating for a culture of peace in a gender perspective, we will observe that these variations, as well as the understanding that concepts of gender and views of gender roles, like all other aspects of culture, are living evolving qualities. Change is a fundamental attribute of all life.

• Foundational concepts

This course of study, as indicated, is constructed on the basis of particular concepts which have been developed within the field of peace education. In order to assure that those following the course have the necessary grasp of the concepts on which it is based, a summary list of key concepts is provided at the end of each section for review and integration into the discussions and demonstration teachings that should comprise class procedures for the course. Students should keep learning journals in which to record their own reflections on the core content, its gender implications and what they are learning from the readings, class discussions and exercises.

One section of the journal should be devoted to the foundational concepts and how they might be integrated into the type of teaching they are preparing to do. Task groups could be formed to discuss and plan learning units based on selected concepts deemed most essential to the students' expected teaching situations. Here the discussion should centre on why the selected concepts are most relevant, and what the potential relevance of gender to teaching the concepts in their expected situations may be.

• Violence

In peace education violence is considered to be avoidable, intentional harm, inflicted for a purpose or perceived advantage of the perpetrator or of those who, while not direct perpetrators, are, however, advantaged by the harm. The structural violence of unequal access to social benefits and resources is one example of such harm. To most forms of violence there are usually alternative non-violent means to achieve the ends sought by the perpetrators. Violence is not an inevitable or immutable element in human life and society, as has been asserted by scientists in the Seville Statement on Violence [7].

• Non-violence

Non-violence is the principle of doing no harm. The principle is the core of a fundamental social philosophy that holds 'truth force' to be more ethical and effective than 'brute force'. This philosophy is the basis of a system of action for social, political and economic change. Peace scholar Gene Sharp has identified 198 tactics for non-violent struggle for justice and social change (see *A Peace Reader: Essential Readings in War, Justice, Non-violence and World Order*, New York, Paulist Press, 1992). In the last decades of the twentieth century, non-violent strategies were employed by major movements for change in many countries.

• Human dignity

This concept is the source of all notions and standards of human rights. It refers to the equal human worth of all persons that is to be universally respected and the responsibility of all to both respect the worth of others and comport ourselves so as to be worthy of

Introduction to education for a culture of peace

respect. Human dignity is manifest in this reciprocal respect and responsibility.

• Cultural diversity

This is a value based upon respect for the multiple manifestations of human objectives, practices, institutions, belief systems, art forms, family structures and gender arrangements in different cultures, ethnic and national groups. It acknowledges that there are many and various ways in which people can express human values and meet human needs.

• Social responsibility

This form of responsibility refers to the readiness and capacity to respond appropriately and effectively to the needs and conditions that face society. In this case the needs and conditions are those of the various communities and societies from local to global to which all planetary citizens are responsible.

• Ecological awareness

This means being mindful that the life-forms of this planet are fragile, irreplaceable and essential to a sustainable environment. It facilitates an understanding of the Earth as a whole, a living system of which humans are an integral part. Such awareness takes into account the effects of all human behaviours and social actions on the natural environment, leading to a sense of environmental responsibility that responds constructively to the consequences of these effects.

• Gender

Gender is a device for classifying and categorizing for linguistic and social purposes. It differentiates between masculine and feminine and has become a common usage term that distinguishes men from women and defines their respective roles. Concepts of masculinity and femininity are defined by cultures. Gender does not refer to the biological but to the social and cultural differences between the sexes. Concepts of gender are fluid and change over time with changing historical and cultural conditions.

• Gender apartheid

This phrase has been used to describe the cases in which rigidly constructed gender roles and severely enforced separation of men and women tend to close women off from a great a range of the benefits of society and limit their influence over society and their capacity to control their own lives. It thus creates a situation of gender oppression similar to the racial oppression of the legal separation of Whites from Blacks that prevailed under apartheid or segregation systems.

• Gender sensitivity

This means being aware of and honouring the differences between men and women and understanding the distinctions between biologically and culturally derived differences, and sensitive to the functions and significance of gender. Such sensitivity leads to awareness of gender inequalities and injustices and to according equal human value to both sexes while honouring their differences.

• Social purposes

These are the ends sought by socially organized groups as determined by their common goals and shared values. Education is a significant means to such ends. Social purposes influence the establishment of learning goals and the designation of instructional objectives. The purpose of this study unit, designed for educators who see themselves as members of the world society, is to assist teachers and teacher educators in educating their respective students about the needs and opportunities for a culture of peace characterized by gender justice.

• Learning goals

The development of the human capacities sought as the intended outcomes of a systematically undertaken educational programme, developmental process or course of study designated as the desired result of these planned learning experiences. The teaching methods proposed at the end of each section are directed towards achieving these goals through particular instructional objectives.

• Instructional objectives

These are the skills and knowledge that make up the intended outcomes of particular teaching methods, lessons or component processes of a curriculum. Course syllabi and study units are usually directed towards general learning goals and individual lesson plans and learning exercises towards particular objectives.

• Mainstreaming

When an issue or concept is seen as crucial to most functions of an institution or society it is taken into account in all spheres of action and policy-making. As applied here, it means taking gender and peace into account throughout the curriculum, in all learning processes and in the formulation of educational policies to assure that they are conducive to the achievement of peace and gender justice.

• War system

The various institutions and processes that maintain military means to defend nations and peoples and achieve national goals by force, if deemed necessary, comprise a war system. Authoritarian and competitive in nature, privileging the military over the civil sector of society in resource allocation, it places military readiness high on the list of political priorities. It perpetuates militarist values, a belief in the inevitability of violence and in the efficacy of coercive force. It is the institutional core of the culture of war and violence.

• Planetary perspective

The integral interdependence among the bioregions and peoples of this planet requires that we see Earth as a whole, looking at any issue or topic in a holistic context that acknowledges that the Earth is a single living system, that all parts of the biosphere are interrelated with all other parts, and that Earth and humanity are interdependent parts of the whole.

• Ecological approach

Some peace educators advocate that a form of organic or ecological thinking should inform teaching for peace. They assert the need to acknowledge that social systems and biological systems are living, therefore changing, and in need of life-sustaining care. It is another dimension of the holistic approach to problem-solving advocated by peace education.

• Learning processes and projects

The learning exercises in this syllabus are presented in forms suitable to learners above 15 years of age. However, some can be adapted for younger learners of elementary-grade level, and all can be adapted for older learners.

Introduction to education for a culture of peace

• Discussion guidelines and a sample procedure

Guidelines

Peace education favours participatory and dialogic forms of pedagogy. Such forms, it is believed, are more effective than traditional, didactic approaches in developing the capacities and skills of discourse necessary to the exploration and solution of the problems that stand as obstacles to a culture of peace. Discussion among students of various ages on topics and at a level of discourse suited to their respective development can be used in most universities and schools of all levels. Where classes are too large to allow for full participation of all, smaller groups may be formed to conduct the discussions. Those preparing to be teachers will need to perfect their skills of discussion leading as a means to facilitate learning for all in the groups. Small groups provide a useful opportunity to practise these skills. Students, in schools as well as teacher-education classes, should take turns leading and reporting the discussions to the entire class.

Discussion leaders should assure that every member of the group is encouraged to participate (but not necessarily required to, especially in first experiences with such groups). They should avoid authoritarian control, viewing their roles as facilitators, assuring that all ideas are articulated and discussed with respect. They should, as diplomatically as possible, dissuade individuals who may (consciously or unwittingly) tend to dominate in the discussion.

Leaders should also encourage and facilitate attentive, reflective listening, so that those who speak are truly heard and understood, and those who listen truly engage in participatory hearing by attending closely and reflecting thoughtfully on what is said. It should be emphasized that both speaking and listening are significant functions of learning in group discussion. Recognizing the equal importance of both functions is important to observing democratic practice and gender sensitivity in the group process.

Principles of equality and democracy should be observed as

important guidelines for constructive discussion groups which contribute to the learning of all as the group seeks to clarify and come to some conclusions about the issues before it. Leaders and facilitators need to be gender sensitive and facilitate equal participation of both male and female participants, especially when the sex ratio is unequal. Gender awareness is another quality important to leading discussions for peace learning with a gender perspective. The leaders and facilitators should enable the group to consider the gender dimensions as well as the peace aspects of all topics discussed. This enablement is, in part, a process of mainstreaming gender and peace.

Reporters should emphasize the conclusions reached and the reasoning that led to the conclusions. Principles of equality, democracy and gender sensitivity should be observed in reaching and reporting conclusions as they are in conducting the discussion. It may be useful to report interesting differences and controversies which arise in the course of reaching conclusions, or presenting the reasons why conclusions were not reached. However, a detailed review of the whole discussion of any group is not usually instructive or interesting to others, except in cases where the discussion process itself is the subject of the report. If the process is reviewed, any gender-related characteristics of the discussion should be accounted for, and in all reports the gender and peace-related arguments and conclusions should be noted for the consideration of the whole class.

Sample procedure

To conduct discussion of the topics and questions below, organize the class into groups of four to seven participants and assign one set of questions to each. Designate one participant in each group to serve as discussion leader/facilitator and one as reporter.

The facilitator presents the discussion questions and helps the group (a) to clarify points made; (b) to challenge, compare and contrast positions taken; (c) to assess arguments, reasons and evidence offered to support positions; (d) to identify ways in which different positions might complement and strengthen each other; and (e) to integrate ideas towards the fullest possible consideration of the topic in the time allowed in order to assist the reporter in summarizing the conclusions and verifying them with the group in preparation for presenting the group report to the entire class.

At the end of the time allowed for the discussion, allow reporters five minutes to present their conclusions and reasons. Participants in other groups should have an opportunity to ask each reporter questions of clarification. Challenges and comparisons of all the groups' conclusions should form the final discussion by the whole class. The instructor should sum up with the main points and identify the most significant learnings that the students should take from the full class discussion to integrate into the overall learning process that comprises this unit or the course of which it is a part.

1. Review the Declaration and Integrated Framework of Action on Education for Peace, Human Rights and Democracy.
    • Which of the statements of objectives seem to you most necessary to educate for a culture of peace, and most adaptable to the situation in which you will be teaching?
    • How would you apply them to a curriculum for your students?
    • Do the statements on educational equality for women seem adequate to the breadth and complexity of gender issues in education?

2. Review the Universal Declaration of Human Rights. What might you suggest as the most appropriate way to open discussion of these rights in the cultural context in which you will be teaching? What are some of the ways in which you can relate the universal human values articulated in the Declaration to some of the particular cultural values of the students you will be teaching? Do you envision that some of them may be problematic? How might you help your students to approach such problems in a manner which is conducive to clear reasoning and critical thinking? How might you lead students through a gender interpretation of the Declaration?

3. Review the Convention on the Elimination of All Forms of
Discrimination against Women (CEDAW). Familiarize yourself
also with the Optional Protocol to the CEDAW. What does the
CEDAW indicate to be the main problems of gender
discrimination against women? Which of these problems do
women in your society experience? Are there ways in which men
in your society experience gender discrimination? How might
you introduce your students to the concept of gender
discrimination?

• Projects

Projects can be subdivided into group tasks and then integrated
into a common class output. Projects are very useful devices for co-
operative learning to teach the social skills of working with others
while increasing the learning of individuals.

Prepare a statement on the rationale and need for
comprehensive, universal education for a culture of peace.
Circulate the statement to other students of education and
professional educators, inviting their endorsing signatures. Send
the signed statement to your Minister of Education, teacher unions
and professional associations requesting publication in their
newsletters and/or journals.

Suggested readings

The readings below and those from 'A Bibliography on the Theory and Practice of Peace Education' [15] can be used by instructors who wish to extend this study unit to a full course.

- **Promoting a Culture of Peace, a Thematic Debate**, (World Conference on Higher Education in the Twenty-first Century: Vision and Action, Vol. 4, Paris, UNESCO, 1998 (ED. 99/HEP/WCHE/Vol. IV.10).)
- **Seville Statement on Violence** [7].
- **Women and Human Rights: The Basic Documents**, (Center for the Study of Human Rights, New York, Columbia University, 1996 (ISBN 1881482-03-0).)
- **Shahra Razavi and Carole Miller**, *Gender Mainstreaming, a Study o the Efforts by the UNDP, World Bank and the ILO to Institutionaliz Gender Issues*, 1995 (ISBN 1020-3354).
- **Hilkka Pietila and Jeanne Vickers**, *Making Women Matter, The Role of the United Nations*, London, Zed Books, 1996 (ISBN 1-85649-458-6).
- **Arundhati Roy**, *The Cost of Living and the End of Imagination*, Modern Library, 1999.

Recommended research

Research can extend and deepen learning on the topic of study while teaching the skills of fact-gathering, analysis and interpretation important to the social and political efficacy this syllabus seeks to promote.

Look into the indices of equality between women and men in your societ in regard to access to: (a) education at all levels; (b) employment opportunities; (c) comparative numbers of men and women in various professions; and (d) comparative numbers of women and men in government and other areas of leadership.

Gather a list of teaching resources related to gender issues in education Try to categorize them by particular issues that may be relevant to the teaching you are preparing to do. Determine how these gender issues need to be taken into account in your teaching and make a plan t do so.

Compare the social with the military expenditures in your country. Note especially the differential between expenditures on the military and those on education. Inquire into the differential in expenditures and opportunities for education that may exist between boys and girls. Ministries of education, UNESCO and UNICEF are good sources for educational data.

Section 2

A culture of peace:
the social and personal dimensions

• Social goals: images of a humane society

The characteristics of any society are derived from the cultures in which they are formed. Societies organize themselves and develop their modes of performing the functions for their continuation as distinct human groups on the basis of what they believe about: (a) the nature of the social and natural worlds; (b) the place and role of human beings in both; and (c) the relationships between human beings and nature, and among human beings similar to and different from themselves. Such beliefs influence the values of a culture. Cultural values affect the social institutions established to perform the functions of making a life, negotiating personal and group identities, and arranging relationships among a society's members.

Culture teaches us who we are, where and what we have come from, what we are to do with our lives and what is important in life. In the stage of oral tradition these instructions were carried in germinal myths, the epic tales which give people their identities and invest their ways of life with meaning. While there are common elements in many of these myths, they are also varied enough to provide a people with a sense of being heirs to unique qualities that are worth struggling to preserve. Recorded histories document the evolutions of peoples, their common experiences and their struggles to realize their unique qualities, keep or expand their places within their environment and among other peoples. A person's culture and the history of his or her people help to provide meaning to life. Meaningful lives are important to individuals' sense of identity and worth, and giving meaning to common experiences binds a people together so as to assure the continuity and survival of the society.

The human species is characterized as much by the fundamental physical and psychological commonalties of universal needs and aspirations as by cultural distinctions and differences of ethnic and national identities. Yet cultures and identities vary so widely, and are so diverse, that they often obscure the commonalties. In our present world the obscuring of the commonalties and the emphasizing of differences has contributed to conflict and has often rationalized violence. Indeed, the phenomenon of moral exclusion, placing persons or groups outside the scope of justice, denying them the claim to full and fair realizations of their human rights, has rationalized crimes as horrific as enslavement and genocide, practices that flourish in a culture of violence. Education for a culture of peace would help us to learn the value of cultural diversity, and how to assure that ethnic plurality flourishes in a common culture of universal human dignity. The assurance of this value is fundamental to the transformation sought by a human-rights approach to education for a culture of peace.

Culture is a powerful factor in human institutions, human relations and human behaviour. Building a culture of peace depends very much on education, because education in our contemporary world is a main carrier of culture. Only education can enable societies to understand the culture of violence which has blighted our past, debases our present and threatens our future. It is through education that the peoples of the world will be able to derive and prepare to pursue the vision of a culture of peace. A positive vision of a peaceful future would be the most effective catalyst to the changes such a future calls on us to make.

The function of a vision is to inspire hope and enlist energies in a movement towards its realization. Visions inform the literature, music and art which articulate the goals of movements such as those for peace, human rights, women's equality and a sustainable environment. Creating, studying, enjoying and performing art give us a deeper understanding of the aspirations and motivations of those who conceived and conduct the movements. On a personal level we often call visions 'dreams', when visualizing something we hope will come to pass. Visions have played an important role in human history. They have moved individuals and societies to undertake great risks and sacrifices. They have informed social and political transformations in human life and society, such as movements for representative government, freedom of worship, abolition of chattel slavery, universal franchise, and the recognition of the human rights of women.

In many cases, violent revolutions and wars were the means by which the changes intended to implement the visions were achieved. But most responsible people today realize that the risks and the costs of violent social change are, and perhaps always were, far too great. Often the vision was betrayed, the values that informed it violated, and the hoped-for transformation aborted. For these practical as well as ethical reasons, non-violence is the conceptual and normative centre of a culture of peace. Thus, non-violent philosophy and practice, including the skills of non-violent direct action are included as main curricular components of education for a culture of peace.

Visions of a culture of peace depict aspirations for non-violent social orders. While abstract, value inspired visions can kindle hope and lead to the contemplation of change, more concrete concepts are necessary to move societies towards social change. Education for a culture of peace must cultivate the imagination and enable learners to envision possibilities for transformation of cultures of violence. To complement the cultivation of the imagination, peace education must also promote the learning of pragmatic skills of planning practical alternatives and designing strategies for their achievement.

It is these practical reasons that have led peace educators to see the usefulness of images, more specific descriptions of the conditions that would realize the values that produce visions of transformation. Such descriptions illuminate the particular nature of the changes essential to the fulfilment of the vision. They are descriptions of changes that can bring about the proposals for policy changes, for strategies to implement them and detailed plans for the reform of existing institutions or the creation of the new institutions which would comprise a transformed international system capable of cultivating a global culture of peace. Such institutional plans are called models. They are proposed by advocates of change who wish to offer a clear understanding of the institutional changes or creations they propose and how these institutions would function. Sometimes these detailed proposals are called draft plans. Draft plans are often developed and circulated to create new treaties and international agreements by individuals or non-governmental organizations (NGOs), international commissions or United Nations Member States. A current NGO plan for disarmament entitled *Global Action to Prevent War* is being circulated throughout the world. The plan is one of a number of such proposals that would make useful material for teachers who seek to introduce the concepts of images and models to their students. Curricular devices for such teaching have also been designed (see Suggested Readings for address on page 66).

What has been lacking in most of these proposals to make them fully and universally in accordance with the basic principle of universal human dignity is a gender perspective. The review and appraisal of all such plans should include this perspective. Guidelines are offered to teachers to enable them to lead their students in a gender review and appraisal process [9].

• Social values of a culture of peace: ethical goals, assessment of present conditions and proposals for change

All social policies, extant and proposed, are based on social values. Policies derived in the interest of the people of a society are expressions of what policy-makers or policy-proposers believe are good and worthy goals and procedures for their societies. They are goals and procedures consistent with the values of the society and the culture or cultures that formed it. Too frequently, however, policies are made in the interest of the policy-makers themselves or those other than the general public to whom they are responsible. Although leaders may claim that their policies are for the common good, policies that are not derived democratically rarely serve the authentic interests of all the people. Thus, UNESCO's Integrated Framework of Action on Education for Peace, Human Rights and Democracy emphasizes education for democracy, noting its varied forms. Democracy is the policy-making method most consistent with a culture of peace.

Policies that do not serve equally the interests of men and women are not truly democratic. Citizens as well as policy-makers must learn how to subject all policy proposals to a gender analysis and include gender justice as one of the main criteria for assessing the fairness of any policy. Democracy also calls for all who are to be affected by a policy to play a role in its formation, from conceptualization to application and assessment. Citizens must be aware of the importance of gender balance in policy- and decision-making, and how to act to assure gender equality. Such learning is essential to the development of social responsibility and political efficacy and should have a central place in formal education.

Social values are the main inspiration of most of the NGO proposals for peace-making, and models of alternative institutions to assure its effectiveness. Every proposal should be analysed for its value content. Some proposals and models openly state the value assumptions that underlie them. One such case was that of the World Order Models Project, UNESCO Peace Education Laureate of 1990. This international peace research project undertaken in the 1970s brought together a group of scholars from all world regions to analyse obstacles to peace and propose alternative international policies and institutions to overcome these problems. They began their work with an extensive inquiry into the elaboration of a set of values that all participating scholars agreed to advocate as consistent with their respective cultures and political systems (socialist and capitalist, industrialized and developing nations were represented.) They identified five core values: peace, social justice, economic equity, political participation and ecological balance. In later years they added positive human identity. However, even these forward-looking scholars did not include gender equality as a fundamental value, believing it to be subsumed under the value of social justice. Consequently, gender did not fit into their problem analysis and did not play a significant role in the proposals the project put forth.

Among other similar cases is the Commission on Global Governance which produced the very valuable report entitled *Our Global Neighborhood* (Report of the Commission on Global Governance, Oxford University Press, 1995). An interesting exercise for those preparing to be educators of future decision-makers would be to do a gender analysis and assessment of these and other such proposals for global change. What is called for here is 'mainstreaming' gender in the conceptualizations and content, not only in the discussion and promulgation, of policy proposals. Gender should always be introduced as a factor in the educational discourse that surrounds the consideration of public policies in educational institutions, most especially in those institutions that are preparing teachers to educate for global citizenship. Main-streaming gender issues and perspectives is important for the realization of the value of gender equality and the achievement of a culture of peace. As such it is integral to education for a culture of peace.

• Social values: applying ethical principles to our daily lives

The two fundamental ethical principles of non-violence and human dignity as they would apply to our own daily lives are enumerated in The UNESCO Manifesto 2000 for a Culture of Peace and Nonviolence [10]. The manifesto indicates that every person can take individual action to live by these principles and in so doing help to bring about the changes that will lead to a more fully humane and peaceful society. It is important for teachers of all grades and subjects to bring the spirit of the manifesto into all their teaching. As asserted above, all peace education should include the concepts and philosophy of non-violence. Perhaps more important than the subject matter would be the modelling of these principles, helping students to develop attitudes and behaviours which manifest the norms and skills of non-violence, maintaining a classroom climate that nurtures the development of the attitudes and behaviours and modelling them in our relationships with students and colleagues. The classrooms, schools and communities in which children and youth are educated and socialized offer many opportunities to practise such forms of non-violence as: non-cooperation with, protest of and resistance to various instances of violence and injustice; intervention to prevent and/or stop the physical, verbal or psychological violence that is perpetrated by the young themselves or members of their communities; personal sacrifice and witness to demonstrate commitment to the non-violent resolution of a conflict or solution to a problem that may affect the classroom, school or community.

The achievement of a gender-just and peaceful classroom climate calls for teacher modelling of the applied principles, evident attitudes and behaviours that manifest gender equality. Just as the principle of non-violence is to be included as subject matter through the introduction of its history, concepts, philosophy and strategies, so, too, gender equality should be addressed in curriculum. Subjects should include the concept of gender roles, characteristics, and how they vary from culture to culture, as well as historical changes in gender roles. Evidence of gender injustice and the history and purposes of women's movements for equality should also be included, especially in the secondary curriculum.

However, it is the gender climate of the classroom that is the most powerful conveyer of attitudes and values of gender equality and justice. In some Western countries there is considerable research on such indicators of gender climate as the comparative amount of attention teachers give to male and female students in the same class, the differential in the number of recitations invited or given by male as compared with female students. In both single-sex and mixed-sex institutions, the differences in offerings that tend to reinforce limiting gender roles and opportunities have been designated as an indicator of inequality. Easier access to education for boys is cited as unjust gender discrimination.

However, the less measurable aspects of teacher attitudes and the psycho-social aspects of the classroom have been less attended to. Yet these are among the primary sources of gender attitudes and behaviours, and they must become central to the preparation for and delivery of education for a culture of peace. Gender tolerance is a fundamental element of respect for human dignity, and as such, is a major learning objective outlined in this syllabus.

• Social possibilities and proposals for peace

Through all the ages of human history people have longed for – and proposed – visions of peace. Many of our religious traditions have thought of their concepts of paradise as visions of peace. Some philosophers described their images of better, even perfect, societies such as the sixteenth-century English work, *Utopia*, by Thomas More. Conquests of others' territories were even declared to have been for the sake of extending peace to these other regions. So human experience of the concept of peace was deemed to be 'other-worldly', meaning something not to be experienced in this life, or 'utopian', meaning not practically possible, or a cynical deception of the populace by leaders who sought not peace but greater power. Those who took seriously the idea that peace was possible and could be achieved if both the 'will' and the 'way' were found were always a tiny minority. While the great majority longed for peace, they did not believe it was truly in the realm of human possibility. Yet the ideas of the minority who set themselves to the task persisted, so that in the twentieth century, called by some 'the bloodiest century in human history', there were, in the midst of constant and multiple wars, 100 years of serious, if flawed, attempts at putting forward proposals espoused by the authors and their supporters as mechanisms to prevent war and maintain lasting peace.

The first of these proposals came at the turn of the century with the establishment of the International Court of Justice, by the Tsar of Russia and the Queen of the Netherlands. The Court was the product of several centuries of Western thought about how law might be brought to bear on the prevention of war as it had been to mitigate its more brutal effects, since 1625, when Grotius published the *Laws of War and Peace*. These latter efforts were codified into International Treaty Law in the Geneva Conventions of 1922. (That the law might be a mode of governing the affairs among nations as it had been within nations was a notion that had been espoused by advocates of peace since the mid-eighteenth century with the publication of Vatell's *The Law of Nations*.) The ethical underpinnings of these legal proposals were to be found in works such as those of the Abbé Saint Pierre and Emmanuel Kant. Kant's *Perpetual Peace* and his advocacy of the 'categorical imperative', which insists that persons must never be perceived or treated as means to the ends of another, profoundly influenced this Western thinking on war and peace and the ethical norms that should apply to the behaviour of nations. These ideas ultimately produced the concept of 'human rights' as it now appears in the international human rights treaties, and stimulated the concept of applying law rather than force to settle international disputes which led to the establishment of the International Court of Justice in The Hague in 1899.

All of these ideas came together with those of other cultures and continents in the international movements for peace and human rights in the twentieth century. There was among these movements recognition that the relations between nations needed to be ordered by institutions dedicated to these same goals. A range of such institutions were established such as the International Labour Organisation, the League of Nations and its successor the United Nations. With the rise of global civil society, the concept of global citizenship became a practical political reality. Two cogent examples of active global citizenship are the World Order Models Project of the 1970s and The Hague Appeal for Peace Civil Society Conference of 1999.

The World Order Models Project grew out of an intense study and evaluation of a proposal for enforceable world law (Grenville Clark and Louis B. Sohn, *World Peace Through World Law*, Cambridge, Mass., Harvard University Press, 1962). It argued for limited world government as a means to prevent and ultimately eliminate war. It comprised carefully detailed proposal aimed to amend the United Nations Charter, provide the world organization with practical capacities for international peacekeeping, and endow the World Court with 'compulsory jurisdiction' – the right to hold violators of the laws of disarmament and peace legally responsible and authorizing the Court to settle disputes that threaten the peace. It was one of a number of plans for world government and/ or strengthening the United Nations to enable it to be as fully effective as possible in its espoused task of eliminating the 'scourge of war'.

These proposals, though extremely problematic primarily because they were drafted from a more western than global perspective, provided inspiration for further thought and useful models for study for researchers, educators, and students. In all world regions, people from many nations and cultures have applied themselves to the task of proposing possibilities for alternative approaches to present problems and impasses that prevent the realization of the long-held visions of and the institutional models for a warless world. With the exception of a number of women's peace groups, however, virtually none of these proposal are drafted from, nor do they even acknowledge, a gender perspective. In recent years the vital interests of women to be affected by the International Criminal Court, established by the Rome Statutes in 1998, would also have been ignored had it not been for the vigilance and effective lobbying of women's NGO groups, notably the Women's Caucus for Gender Justice.

Many who have been involved in the formation and promulgation of such proposals were among those who gathered at The Hague Appeal for Peace Civil Society Conference held to commemorate the centenary of the establishment of the International Court of Justice and to project a vision for the twenty-first century, exploring some of the recent models and proposals for making it the time 'to abolish war'. A number of these proposals were adopted by the conference as The Hague Agenda for Peace and Justice in the 21st Century, an aggregation of specific proposals to limit armaments, reduce militarism, promote the rule of law to settle disputes and hold violators of human rights and other international laws legally responsible [11]. A review of this agenda provides for study and action on a wide range of possibilities to make the struggle for peace more effective and successful.

The Agenda does not attempt to provide an integrated overall plan such as some of the previously noted proposals do. It does not comprise a model but rather certain essential components of a model and specific steps towards the elimination of war. While 'engendering the peace process' is a theme and goal endorsed by the Agenda, the concept does not serve as an integrating factor or comprehensive perspective or framework. This fact makes the Agenda an even more interesting material for study by those preparing to educate for a culture of peace. It provides the working pieces with which educators might practise their own skills for integrating a gender perspective. It also provides components with which to practise model-building. As recounted above, imaging and model-design are significant skills advocated by peace education as it has been developed over recent decades.

• A culture of peace encompasses all levels of human society

Images of a culture of peace can be located in our families, communities, nations, geographical regions and the world. We can describe conditions of peace at all these levels of human society, and could design institutions to maintain peace and assure the fulfilment of the values that lead us to seek such conditions. All relational groups that comprise our various human cultures can be the subject of imaging. We can image how our nuclear and extended families can become carriers of a culture of peace; how our ethnic groups can come to embrace the fundamental ethical principles and manifest the universal values that would infuse a global culture of peace. We can propose interpretations of our religious scriptures and modes of worship that uphold peace and universal human dignity. We can sketch out institutional changes for our municipalities, nations and regional organizations which would enhance the values and assure the human rights that we know to be the base of a culture of peace. We can institute learning processes in all these spheres and levels of human society and culture, leading us to examine which of their characteristics are consistent with a culture of peace and which may need to be changed so as not to impede the learning about and striving for peace. Imaging in all these spheres can be the substance of peace curricula.

None of these possibilities, no matter what sphere or level, can be fulfilled without establishing the value base for the development of a range of human capacities for initiating and maintaining humane relationships and engaging in constructive citizenship. Such values and capacities can and should be developed through systematically planned education for a culture of peace. Such education should be delivered in a manner consistent with the core ethical principles, values and norms of a culture of peace, manifesting the values of environmental sustainability, social responsibility and gender equity.

Foundational concepts

Culture

Culture comes from the same root as 'cultivate', meaning to grow or develop. It means both the arts and skills of a people and all the ways they have devised to mediate/express the human experience. People themselves devise and develop their cultures. The culture of war has been devised and developed by human beings, and human beings can devise and develop a culture of peace.

Gender bias

Such bias, sometimes referred to as sexism, is still widespread throughout the world. It is the attitude that underlies gender discrimination. Gender bias is the attitude that holds that men and women are not equally capable of performing the same social, political and economic tasks and functions. The bias divides tasks and functions into those for which men are suited and those most appropriate for women. It is a form of prejudice that often makes women invisible to planners and policy-makers. Thus, women continue to remain outside most spheres of political power, economic management and much of the public realm. Men are seldom found in caring work, community organizations and work in the home. Such conditions are made evident when the statistics used for planning, policy making and assessing economic and political participation are disaggregated by sex.

• Gender tolerance

Gender tolerance, in contrast to gender bias, rejects such bias in favour of opening all opportunities not biologically determined to both men and women. It is an attitude that accepts men in spheres traditionally occupied by women such as childcare and home maintenance and of women in work and public areas occupied by men, such as the sciences and politics. Men cannot breast-feed infants, but they can prepare meals for children. Most women (and many men) cannot lift huge and heavy construction components, but they can operate lifting equipment.

• Gender differences

These are culturally derived and socially contextualized differences between men and women, as contrasted with biologically based physical differences. Such differences are designated as masculine for men and feminine for women. Masculine and feminine characteristics are usually seen as oppositional, such as strong/weak, and assertive/compliant.

• Gender responsibility

This means responding to gender differences so as to assure equal respect to men and women and just treatment to both sexes, and standing against gender bias.

- ## Humane

These are behaviours and institutions that reflect human responsibility to honour human dignity and respect for living creatures and systems.

- ## Humanity

This is the characteristic of being human and also the collective of all human beings as a single ethical unit with rights and responsibilities.

- ## Vision

Vision is an imagined, value informed, generalized idea of a possible future or alternative reality which inspires action for change. The idea of a culture of peace is a vision.

- ## Image

This is a conceptual tool and heuristic device for depicting something that one believes is possible, words or artistic descriptions of something different from present or projected reality or which informs the way we interpret reality. Our images influence how we think things are or could be. Positive images usually produce positive views of both the world's creative and human potential, which encourage constructive action.

- ## Model

A model can be a replica or specified plan for something new, such as plans for constructing institutions to achieve and maintain a disarmed or warless world that would fulfil the vision of a culture of peace. Models can be constructed, drawn, dramatized and communicated in various ways.

A culture of peace: the social and personal dimensions

- ## Monitoring

This refers to citizens' reviewing and reporting how responsible authorities fulfil commitment to social and political goals such as Member States fulfilling international agreements on human rights and gender equality.

- # Learning processes and projects

- ## Process

Imaging a preferred future

The transformation envisioned in the United Nations Declaration and Programme of Action on a Culture of Peace will be the fruit of human imagination and creativity. The development of these capacities is seen by the Integrated Framework of Action on Education for Peace, Human Rights and Democracy as an important objective of education. Teachers can cultivate imagination and creativity in some of the ways advocated in this text, but they need to practise some of the techniques for doing so. One of the most effective of these is 'futures imaging', a process described in some detail in Elise Boulding's book, *Building a Global Civic Culture* (See Suggested Readings on page 66 below). The process outlined here is developed from the same principles, adapted for instructional purposes of education for a culture of peace in a gender perspective.

Procedures

1. Form task groups to function according to the directions in the previous section for group discussion. Apply the guidelines set forth in Section 1 for small group discussion and reporting to the entire class.

2. During the first discussion session of about thirty minutes, all groups should address the task of describing the characteristics

and conditions of a culture of peace in terms of what an ordinary day would be like for a man or a woman in some part of the world. The instructor should assign to each group the sex of the subject of the imaging and region to be addressed so that both male and female lives and various world regions will be included: that is, Group 1 describes a man in eastern Europe, Group 2 a woman in West Africa, etc. They should describe two elements: (a) how the person spends his or her day over a twenty-four-hour period; and (b) what they are likely to read in print or hear through broadcast news. Specify that it would be a day without violence and a life of gender equality, and that the news stories must reflect such conditions. Do they envision social or political problems in a peaceful, gender-just society? What kinds of conflicts might be reported in the news?

3. Ask each group to report by describing the day and the main news stories. Point out the similarities and differences in the groups' images of gender roles and non-violence in a culture of peace. Ask for reflections and comments on these differences and similarities and what might be learned from them that would be helpful in producing images that could teach about the real possibilities for a culture of peace and gender equality.

4. Call for reports on the news stories and the changes that must have occurred in the world to make such stories possible.

5. Ask all to think about the following points to be discussed in the next round of 'imaging':
   A. What kinds of public institutions would be needed to make such a day and such news possible? Describe the institutions, how they function, who runs them and how people become managers of such institutions (government, business, education, etc.).
   B. What changes would have to occur in gender roles and relations to achieve the equality the groups envisioned? Describe how these changes might occur and what particular

responsibilities for change men and women, respectively, would have to assume.

C. What political and economic changes would be necessary to achieve the institutional changes the groups described?

D. What changes would be required in education to enable men and women to carry their respective responsibilities for changes to achieve gender equality?

6. At the beginning of the next class period assign to each group Points A and C or B and D. Thus each group will address and report on two related questions. Discuss for forty minutes. Remind the groups after fifteen minutes that they should now be addressing the second question. At the end of thirty minutes announce that there remain ten minutes to summarize for reporting.

7. After reports, discuss how the changes that have been planned could be integrated into a general strategy for change. For next session students should prepare a 'Declaration of Change for Peace and Gender Justice', a plan of action and a time-line for implementing the action. This should be a written assignment to be submitted for review by the instructor.

8. Have students read their declarations aloud and discuss their plans of action. Then discuss how this exercise could be adapted to upper elementary and secondary schools and what learning objectives they would propose for such adaptations.

Variations

If time does not allow for holding all group discussion during class hours, students could be asked to use class preparation time to meet for these discussions outside class and limit class time to the reports and discussions of the reports.

Images and descriptions of the preferred futures could be presented in alternative ways such as drawings, dramatic sketches, dance, simulated broadcast programmes and various other forms of creative expression.

• Projects

Contact one of the major groups or organizations working for peace and/or gender justice such as The Hague Appeal for Peace or Global Action for Peace, Women's International League for Peace and Freedom, International Fellowship of Reconciliation, Girl Scouts/Girl Guides, and so on. Request information about their work and samples of the literature they distribute. Review this literature for possible use as curricular material. If some of the literature is adaptable, prepare a lesson plan for its use with the students you expect to teach. Analyse it for the values and visions that inform their stated purposes and the potential effectiveness of the actions and strategies they advocate for achieving their purposes. How would you use these materials to teach about global civil society and proposals for global change?

Suggested readings

- **The Hague Agenda for the 21st Century**, United Nations Document: R
  A/54/98 available from The Hague Appeal for Peace, 777 United Nations
  Plaza, New York, NY 10017, 1999.
- **Global Action to Prevent War**, one of the campaigns included in The
  Hague Agenda, materials available from World Order Models Project,
  475 Riverside Drive, New York, NY 10115.
- Elise Boulding, **Building a Global Civic Culture**, New York, Teachers
  College Press, 1985.
- **Building a Culture of Peace**, Canadian Commission for UNESCO,
  350 Albert Street, Box 1047, Ottawa, ON, K1P 5V8, 1999.
- **Creating a Culture of Peace**, a Workshop Kit, Canadian Voice of Wome
  for Peace, (761 Queen St.W., Suite 203, Toronto, Ontario, M6J 1G1) 1998
- Federico Mayor, **The New Page**, Paris, UNESCO, 1995.
- Michael True, **Ordinary People: Family Life and Global Values**,
  Maryknoll, N.Y., Orbis Books, 1991.
- Riane T. Eisler and Nel Noddings, **Tomorrow's Children: A Blueprint fo
  Partnership Education in the 21st Century**, Boulder, Westview Press,
  1, 2000.
- Fredrik S. Heffermehl, **Peace is Possible**, Oslo, International Peace Burea
  2000.
- **Women Say No to War**, Paris, UNESCO Publishing, 1999.

Recommended research

Research the history of concepts and images of peace and more humar
societies, reviewing such works as those of Plato, Thomas More, the Ab
Saint Pierre, Karl Marx, Alexandra Kollontay, Grenville Clark and Louis
Sohn, the World Order Models Project, among others.

Section 3

Human capacities to be developed in education for a culture of peace

Preparatory readings

- **Global Citizenship: A Draft Declaration** [12].
- **Tolerance – The Threshold of Peace,** Unit 3, Chapters 1, 2, 3, pp. 13–20, dealing with indicators for classroom assessment and learning realms in a process approach. (Available from UNESCO Publishing, 7 place de Fontenoy, 75352 Paris 07 SP, France.)
- **Guidelines for a Gender Perspective and Indicators of Gender Tolerance** [9].
- **Betty A. Reardon, Excellence in Education Through Peacemaking,** *The Journal of Global Education, Breakthrough,* Spring/Summer 1987 [13].

• Personal capacities: forming humane persons

The International Commission on Education for the Twenty-first Century advocates as one of its four pillars, 'learning to be' (International Commission on Education for the twenty-first Century (1996) *Learning: The Treasure Within*) [6]. Learning to be human is the result of education of the whole person, and in the case of education for a culture of peace in a gender perspective calls for forming gender-sensitive peace-makers, referred to here as 'humane persons'. Peacemaking capacities, as outlined in the preparatory reading 'Excellence in Education Through Peacemaking' (published in 1987) have long been advocated as learning goals of traditional peace education [13]. Such capacities are but one set among the far broader range of human capacities brought into play when we consider preparing persons to be makers of the very foundation of peace, a culture of peace.

Developing the capacities necessary for bringing forth a culture of peace, calls for the formation of persons committed to and capable of envisioning, designing and constructing alternatives to the present culture of violence. This means, the central concern of the entire educational enterprise and sequence should be the nurturing of humane, peaceful persons. The formation of such persons is to lay the human foundation of the transformed culture.

Many of the great schemes for social or political transformation have predicated their achievability on the formation of a new citizen. Clearly any society is the sum of its members and its qualities are their qualities. Consequently, the paramount goal of education for a culture of peace is the formation of humane and peaceful persons. Such persons were well described by the previous Director-General of UNESCO when he advocated that we teach our children and youth to be

> people with a sense of openness and comprehension towards other people, their diverse cultures and histories and their fundamental shared humanity; [who understand] the importance of refusing violence and adopting peaceful means for resolving disagreements and conflicts; [who manifest] feelings of altruism, openness and respect towards others, solidarity and sharing based on a sense of security in one's own identity and a capacity to recognize the many dimensions of being human in different cultural and social contexts [Federico Mayor, Preface to Betty A. Reardon, *Tolerance – The Threshold of Peace*, Paris, UNESCO Publishing, 1997].

We also see in the Universal Declaration of Human Rights a view of the human person that articulates the philosophical basis of a belief in the fundamental humanity and equality of all human persons.

Article 1. All human beings are born free and equal in dignity and rights. They are endowed with reason and conscience and should act towards one another in a spirit of brotherhood [and we would add, sisterhood].

Article 2. Everyone is entitled to all the rights and freedoms set forth in this Declaration, without distinction of any kind, such as race, colour, sex, language, religion, political or other opinion, national or social origin, property, birth or other status. . . .

Neither of the philosophical premises expressed in these two articles can be realized without an education and enculturation that acknowledges their essentiality to human welfare and a peaceful society. Furthermore it must be recognized that the premise of the first article determines the enactment of the second. Education for a culture of peace must emphasize the development of the capacity to reason, the exercise of conscience and the manifestation of a spirit of human kinship. It must cultivate knowledge of what constitutes justice and the rights that have been identified as the carriers of justice. Human-rights education is, therefore, an effective route to the development of the humanity of persons and their societies.

The formation of humane persons is certainly affected by the content and foundational values of their education. However, even more significant to the formation process is the atmosphere in which and the persons by whom the curriculum is delivered. Section 6 will deal more directly with the capacities and qualities that equip teachers to be educators for peace. Here, we wish to emphasize that the teacher is the delivery agent not only of the curriculum, but of a set of attitudes, a system of values and social priorities that reflect the personal attributes of the teacher and the cultural attributes of the society. Teachers need to be aware of their own and their societies' attributes and values so that they can develop in themselves those necessary to contribute to the formation of humane persons.

The relationships between students and teachers and the relationships teachers encourage among students are the most significant of all the factors involved in education for the formation of humane persons. Humane persons of the type described above by UNESCO's Director-General are nurtured in an atmosphere in which they are treated with dignity and sensitivity, by a teacher who manifests equal respect for the human dignity of all and sensitivity to the diverse personal qualities and capacities of individuals. Gender sensitivity is integral to respect for human dignity and to the development of persons who will strive for gender equality in society. Insistence on the practical observation of universal human dignity in the classroom is the preamble to citizen action to realize human dignity throughout society.

• Relationship capacities

The quality of human lives is largely determined by human relationships; the close personal relationships with friends and family, social relationships with those who share our gender, ethnicity and/or nationality, our neighbours, workmates, schoolmates, co-religionists, members of the organizations, associations and political parties to which we belong and those with whom we come in casual, public or anonymous contact; even those we may never see or know of. Our worlds are made up of self and others, familiars and strangers. The others in our lives are broad and varied. We always have been well aware of how our attitudes and behaviours affect those with whom we spend our days and how they, in turn, affect our own lives. But only in the twentieth century have we come to understand how far these effects extend, how vast and varied are the others with whom we share this one planet on which we all depend.

For decades some schools have been teaching the concept of global interdependence in relationship to political and economic relationships between nations, and more recently about how environmental problems demonstrate ecological interdependence. There has also been a significant movement in intercultural, cross-cultural and multicultural education. What we have not been teaching is the nature and significance of people-to-people relationships, and the many positive possibilities these relationships are opening for collaboration towards the achievement of a culture of peace.

We have not taught either in any depth how to relate to others who are culturally different, assuming that teaching about the history, traditions, beliefs and practices of other cultures is adequate educational response to this challenge. Although some attention has been given to the growing concern for the human rights of women, the construction and cultivation of complementary, humanly enriching gender relationships has also been sorely lacking in school curricula. Mutually enhancing, complementary and co-operative relationships cannot be based on cognitive knowledge alone. Achieving this also involves attitudes, perspectives and skills. Educators for a culture of peace will have to develop the teaching capacities to help students to acquire these attitudes and perspectives and to learn these skills. Some suggested learning processes to realize such educational objectives are offered throughout this syllabus.

Thus far, this narrative has alluded to the importance of tolerance, openness to difference, appreciation of diversity and respect for human dignity. In this discussion of the relationship capacities that underlie some of the learning objectives of education for a culture of peace, these capacities need to be specified for purposes of planning learning processes designed to achieve them. As particular capacities are identified, the significance of gender to each should be noted. Those pursuing this course of study will want to reflect on other dimensions of the suggested definitions and other aspects of the gender implications from the perspectives of their own cultures and schooling practices.

There are, of course, a broad range of such capacities, and educators are urged to augment and reinterpret as needed the suggestions presented here. Most of the following capacities are those involved in relating to differences, to encountering others or 'the other' or strangers. They encompass relating to other persons' customs and behaviours, ways of thinking and ways of managing their societies, that is, cultures, world views and ideologies, social and political systems. The relevant capacities might be enumerated as: (a) tolerance of differences in any of the areas where people may differ, even conflict; (b) appreciation of and ability to view human diversity in terms of complementarity; and (c) moral inclusion, considering those who are different and with whom we differ as being within the realm of justice and deserving of fair treatment.

Tolerance of difference is a capacity that lends itself to cultivation in the classroom. Tolerance as a value and learning objective is treated at some length in UNESCO's three-volume series, *Tolerance – The Threshold of Peace* (1997) which identifies tolerance as a 'threshold' capacity or value which opens the way to the development of higher-order capacities leading to the more fully complementary and mutually enhancing relationships of a truly peaceful community. The concept of a 'threshold' capacity is important to the unfolding of processes of cultural and social change and to the development of more mature relationship capacities. There are various other works in peace education that deal with creating a peaceful climate in the classroom, a number of them cited in these three volumes.

The focus in this course of study, attempting to mainstream gender, is on applying the gender dimension to the broader concept of tolerance as a quality that can lead to a higher order of peaceful gender relations. Peace educators who have studied gender as a factor in the conceptualization and construction of peace believe that gender tolerance is of primary importance as persons of the other sex are, for many, their first experience of 'other'. Teachers need to have means of working with students – both young children and adolescents – in ways that will enable both sexes to respect the other and accept differences between them, in the same way that they are encouraged to respect other cultures and accept as equally valued members of the classroom community students of all ethnic, racial, cultural or religious background. Persons who are gender tolerant and gender sensitive are likely to manifest tolerance of other differences and to be able to develop a mature appreciation for diversity. The Processes and Projects suggested at the end of this section are offered as a way of helping educators to think about methods and strategies for establishing and maintaining a gender-tolerant classroom as the basis for the development of the broader capacities of moral inclusion essential to constructive global citizenship in a planetary culture of peace.

• Appreciation of cultural diversity is manifest in humane persons

Diversity in all its forms is thought by many to be the key to the humanely constructed world social order and the sustainable natural environment that would be the foundations of a planetary culture of peace. Yet diversity in our present world is often seen as inconsequential to the environment and threatening to the cultural integrity or political autonomy of some peoples. Cultural differences are often the rationalization of conflicts and are used to divide and alienate peoples from each other. Some respond to this by insisting that such differences are insignificant compared with human similarities. Others insist that culture is what most defines human beings and that overlooking the differences denies people their full human dignity and identity. These are certainly issues to be explored, and would make useful discussions for students in upper-secondary and post-secondary education. The issues might be explored in terms of the role of cultural diversity in the building of a culture of peace. However, the teacher needs to be able to understand the truth in both arguments; the observance of human universals as the basis of universal human dignity and rights, and respect for cultural difference as a source of human identity. The teacher must also assure that both views, universality of human dignity and diversity of cultures that form unique human identities, are heard with respect and reflection.

Reflective capacities are essential to all forms of learning and to authentic inquiry into all issues and topics studied in education for a culture of peace. Reflection on the questions of human universality and cultural diversity can also help to clarify aspects of gender and deepen understanding of both the complexities and the possibilities of bringing cultural and gender perspectives to the task of learning to build a culture of peace.

Reflection on human universals is important for understanding the principles upon which human-rights standards have been constructed. Here, too, biological facts play a role in clarifying the issues. The science of biology has concluded that humanity is one animal species with the same fundamental physical characteristics and survival needs. Psychology asserts that there are also some fundamental similarities in human emotional response. Humans share similar forms of pleasure, joy, pain and suffering. The core purpose of human-rights standards is to prevent the pain and suffering that some humans cause or permit in others.

Other human sciences also illuminate cultural similarities in most human groups. Sociologists note that all groups have institutions for governance, marriage and family, religious belief and resource allocation. Anthropologists have observed that most human groups have their own myths of origin, a common views of the world, shared practices of worship, a common language, traditional practices of child-rearing, particular ways of preparing food and particular definitions of gender and gender roles. Human groups demonstrate that the functions of culture are similar while the forms are very different, demonstrating the human capacity to devise various ways of meeting the same basic needs of fulfilling similar social and cultural functions. Human beings adapt social institutions and cultural forms to their environments as well as to their perceptions of their needs and the possibilities of fulfilling them. The great variety in environments and possibilities produces a great variety of cultural forms. Understanding these factors leads not only to an appreciation of human adaptability and creativity but also to the realization that because cultures derive from such a wide range of circumstances, they cannot be evaluated so as to say one is superior to another. Ethnocentrism and assertions of cultural superiority derive largely from lack of knowledge of the origins of cultures and the conditions in which they evolved.

In teaching for appreciation of cultural diversity teachers can use the human sciences, especially anthropology, to see the differences in culture in positive terms of the variety of possibilities they offer for creating a culture of peace. They can also teach how cultures have evolved and adapted to the circumstances of the people who have created a particular culture. Students can be helped to understand that cultures are constructed, not given, that they change and evolve according to what the people of the culture see as necessary and possible. In such a discussion the students can be called upon to reflect on what they themselves see as the need and possibilities for a culture of peace.

With such understanding of the evolution as well as the characteristics of various cultures, students should be better able to develop capacities for positive and enriching cross-cultural relationships whether they take place in the classroom or in the world at large. Education for the appreciation of cultural diversity can also be a basis for promoting a deeper understanding of gender and its origins in culture. By emphasizing cultural differences in gender roles and attributes, educators can demonstrate to students that gender is not biological. It does not fall in the physical realm as do universal basic needs. Indeed, it is more varied and more subject to human determination than some other cultural characteristics. Tracing the changes in gender roles is a useful way to demonstrate cultural evolution, illustrate possibilities for all cultures to become more gender equal and more peaceful, and show the relationships between gender equality and peace.

Such inquiries and reflections must also take note of some of the negative aspects of cultural relativism that have been used to rationalize conditions and practices that are violations of universal human rights. The Beijing Platform for Action (1995) [14] states that such practices when they perpetrate gender injustice and gender violence should be considered and dealt with as human rights violations. The signatories to the UNESCO Statement on Women's Contribution to a Culture of Peace (1995) commit

Human capacities to be developed in education for a culture of peace

themselves to 'oppose the misuse of religion, cultural and traditional practices for discriminatory purposes'.

Moral inclusion: a primary attribute of a humane person

Understanding these differences and the factors that condition them can contribute to developing a capacity for positive human relationships. This capacity is absolutely essential to the achievement of the goals of the international standards on human rights, of social justice, gender justice and all forms of moral inclusion. Ethnocentrism, racism, xenophobia and the various forms of rejections and denigration of others usually result in moral exclusion as defined earlier. A global culture of peace would involve all the peoples of the earth and include them in the universal realm of justice implied in the human-rights standards. Relationship capacities for such a culture depend upon the cultivation of a sense of moral inclusion and the active repudiation of any form of moral exclusion.

Developing an inclusive view of the realm of justice is a learning goal that can be incorporated into the curriculum. It should be intentionally built into the atmosphere of the classroom, modes of teaching and the relationships among students and between students and teachers. In teaching towards the goal of moral inclusion, lessons on the limits of tolerance and the often fine line between tolerance and intolerance can be advanced. As stated in the UNESCO curricular guides on tolerance, human rights are the index of tolerance. Any behaviour or practice that denies or violates human rights is intolerant. Tolerance in the sense of forbearance cannot be extended to such acts. This imperative sets guidelines for teachers to enable them to judge when an intervention in cases or conditions of intolerance or moral exclusion may be necessary. Specific criteria for the assessment of the tolerant classroom and recognizing moral exclusion and intolerance also appear in the three volumes on tolerance. Gender has been as much a factor as racism and ethnocentrism in moral exclusion. For this reason, we offer in the Supplementary materials on p. 195 some of the criteria for a tolerant classroom as outlined in *Tolerance – The Threshold of Peace* adapted to gender (hereafter referred to as *Tolerance*).

Gender awareness and gender sensitivity are crucial elements in the range of relationship capacities required of all global citizens and for all who seek to contribute to the evolution of a culture of peace. Gender relations can be viewed as a paradigm for relating to those who are different. If from early childhood children experience an environment in which both girls and boys are perceived and treated as being of equal worth, they will receive the message that human difference does not carry with it unequal human value. Gender discrimination can also be used as a metaphor for other separations and divisions between people and world regions. As will be outlined in Section 5, gender is a lens that allows a clearer and fuller view of many of the global issues and human problems that stand in the way of a culture of peace. Therefore, gender awareness and gender sensitivity are capacities essential to positive, mutually enhancing relationships and serve to develop deeper understanding of global issues. If teachers can cultivate mutually enhancing gender relationships in the classroom, they can contribute to the formation of global citizens as they strive to develop among their students an appreciation for human diversity.

Gender awareness refers to the capacity to observe and honour the differences between men and women, to distinguish between the differences that are biologically based and those that derive from culture, society and experience, and to understand when these differences are the bases for discrimination and/or moral exclusion.

Gender sensitivity involves both gender awareness and the capacity to respond constructively to the negative consequences to both men and women as they experience gender discrimination and exclusion, calling upon a repertoire of social and political skills to change the discriminatory conditions and work towards gender justice and inclusion. These skills are essentially skills of non-violent action for social change. Categories of skills as related to the realization of the capacities discussed here will be explored more fully in a subsequent section.

• Political capacities: learning to take democratic responsibility for a peaceful public order

Schools in many countries have been charged with the responsibility of educating for citizenship. This has mostly been education regarding the organization of government and citizens' rights and responsibilities, often limited to cognitive knowledge rather than the development of capacities for carrying out those responsibilities and protecting the rights. Such education is usually limited to the nation-state and its components, with little or no attention to issues of world citizenship other than those undertaken by peace educators and teachers involved in UNESCO's Associated Schools Programme. Some school texts have introduced the mission and work of the United Nations, but even that has been marginal to education for national citizenship.

Education for national citizenship is a basic component for the development of political capacities. Every schoolchild should be made thoroughly familiar with his or her government, how it functions, what it expects of its citizens and what its citizens can expect from it. The fulfilment of the respective expectations of states and citizens makes for the kind of mutuality from which democracies are derived. States are established to serve the welfare of the people. The citizen–state relationship is also one that must be mutually enhancing if active citizenship is to be significant in bringing about a culture of peace. Thus, the emphasis of citizen education for a culture of peace is on developing capacities for informed, responsible political action.

In a democracy, the state expects citizens to obey its laws and support its policies, and citizens expect the laws to be just and fashioned so as to serve all citizens with due regard to their human dignity and equality. They expect government policies to reflect the will and best interests of the people. Citizens also have the responsibility to persuade their governments to change unjust laws and unfair or destructive policies. When governments ignore or refuse democratically pursued changes in unjust laws or dysfunctional policies, responsible citizens often refuse to observe the laws, peacefully resisting their enforcement or engaging in other non-violent means of dissent such as demonstrations, campaigns and hunger strikes. A variety of strategies such as these were used by such citizens' initiatives as the women's suffrage movement, the Indian independence movement, the anti-apartheid movement and various civil rights movements. They have even brought down governments which no longer had the support of the people, and more often are the means through which citizens seek to prevent or end violent conflict, sometimes even placing themselves between opposing armed forces. As wars and weapons become more destructive and dehumanized, more and more citizens and some policy-makers are considering the practical possibilities of non-violence.

One of the most contested areas in contemporary politics is the issue of equality, what it should mean in practice and how far it should extend. Discussion of such issues and the changes, legal and other, that would be required to achieve it is very important if gender is to be adequately factored into political education. If we accept the basic principles of the Universal Declaration of Human Rights, all people are equal, including and especially men and women. It must be emphasized that 'equal' cannot be construed as 'the same'. Valuing diversity would make this self-evident. But that does not seem to be the case in discussions of gender equality. Some assert that women's claim to equality is a statement that they see themselves, or want to be the same, as men. This is a misinterpretation of equality. Equality means being the subject of the same universal rights and having access to the same benefits as others, not being culturally, psychologically or physically the same. Rights such as access to education, voting, travelling, employment and property should not be denied on the basis of sex (nor of ethnicity, race, religion or other human differences). Neither should benefits such as health-care, education and cultural opportunities be limited on the basis of human differences. These are the ethical principles that underlie legal assurances of equality.

In pursuing changes in laws and policies, citizens often differ in their approaches and in the particular forms their common political goals should take. In some cases political differences have led to violent conflict within nations, destroying the peace and the wellbeing of the people. Achieving peaceful change and maintaining peaceful, democratic orders requires, as noted above, non-violent skills of resistance and change. A capacity needed even more frequently is that of non-violent conflict resolution. As will be elaborated in the section on social skills, a broad repertoire for dealing constructively with conflict is an essential component of education for a culture of peace. Peace educators and practitioners of conflict resolution believe that the broader the range of such skills and the more adept citizens are at using them, the less likely are outbreaks of violence.

The need for the requisite knowledge and skills to peacefully change conditions of injustice is observed in the Integrated Framework of Action on Education for Peace, Human Rights and Democracy (Paris, UNESCO, 1994, p. 2, paragraph 7):

> Education must develop the ability to value freedom and the skills to meet its challenges. This means preparing citizens to cope with difficult and uncertain situations and fitting them for personal autonomy and responsibility. Awareness of personal responsibility must be linked to recognition of the value of civic commitment, of joining together with others to solve problems and to work for a just, peaceful and democratic community.

Monitoring governments' own compliance with laws and fulfilment of policies is another significant responsibility of democratic citizenship. Such actions often lead to citizens' statements, reminding governments of their obligations, urging them to make needed changes before it becomes necessary to embark on measures of organized dissent and/or undertake non-violent resistance. Groups of citizens organized for such purposes are sometimes called 'watchdog committees' or watch groups such as those established by Human Rights Watch to monitor the violations of the rights in a region, of particular groups of people or of a specific set of the international standards. One such group is the International Women's Rights Action Watch (IWRAW). In order to enable more ordinary citizens to monitor compliance with the Convention on the Elimination of All Forms of Discrimination Against Women (CEDAW), IWRAW prepared and distributed a condensation of the Convention which could be read and used by all literate people. A fundamental necessity of education to develop political capacities is materials such as these that make the various documents containing internationally derived and agreed standards and principles accessible to all citizens. The References to this study unit suggest a number of such documents for curricular use.

Another device through which citizens can directly register concerns at the world level is the Shadow Reports submitted over recent years to the United Nations Division for the Advancement of Women. These reports prepared by non-governmental organizations are supplements to governmental reports on compliance with obligations contracted under CEDAW which are reviewed by the monitoring committee in their annual sessions. They often address topics other than those covered in the governmental reports and sometimes have moved governments to be more exigent in efforts to achieve gender equality.

Shadow reports are manifestations of a most significant world development. The last decades of the twentieth century saw the emergence of global civil society as an important influence in international decision-making. Citizens from all regions of the world banded together to work in co-operation for the achievement of such common goals as environmental standards, eliminating violence against women, and the outlawing of land-mines. Much of the work that convinced the United Nations to mainstream gender in its programmes and policies was done by non-governmental organizations and women's movements which have been an energizing force in global civil society. It is in the rapidly expanding and ever stronger global civil society that the concept of world citizenship is now being realized. So evident and important has it become that students themselves are now calling for more systematic education for world citizenship. Such a call was issued by a global group of secondary-school students at a conference of international schools in October 1999 in *Global Citizenship: A Draft Declaration* [12].

> On the dawn of the twenty-first century, schools assuming the role as 'Agents of Change' need a set of guiding principles to help determine the skills and actions of the new Global Citizen. This document is based upon the principles of Democracy, Human Rights, and Peace Education to encourage in the individual greater awareness and allow him or her to realize the potential consequences of his or her actions. These guiding principles should inspire and guide the generation of tomorrow to take action [The Foundation of the International School of Geneva's Seventy-fifth Anniversary Conference, *Global Citizenship: A Draft Declaration*, October 1999].

The students also presented their own definition of global citizenship.

> The global citizen is someone who: is aware of the wider world and has a sense of their own role as a world citizen; is willing to act to make the world a more equitable and sustainable place; takes responsibility for their actions; respects and values diversity [ibid.].

The Declaration outlines guiding principles for schools cast under the priorities of UNESCO's Integrated Framework of Action on Education for Peace, Human Rights, and Democracy. It then enumerates the skills necessary to function constructively as a global citizen. It is a document that should be considered by every educator who wishes to contribute to the preparation of their students for a culture of peace, for it gives voice to the concerns of the young.

• Economic capacities: learning to contribute to the well-being of self, family and society

The exercise of democratic responsibility in a world in which citizens act at all levels of political organization from the local community to (and including) international systems, calls for a range of capacities beyond the political, most especially, capacities in a realm closely related to politics, and economics. This, too, is a realm in which citizens need to understand how economies function at all levels, the criteria by which economic decisions are made and the gender-related consequences/gender impact of economic policies. In traditional societies most members learned and understood the economy through their daily experience with productive activity and from their places in the system of production. There have been times in history when the arrangements of the system of production were unfair, to the advantage of one or several segments of society over others in conditions we would now recognize as structural violence. In some cases these conditions were changed by political actions, frequently violent action. Today we must educate so as to provide a broad enough range of skills, so that even in the most unjust set of economic circumstances, violence is never necessary. We must also educate to the fact that economic activity is social activity; that an individual's work while providing for self and family also has consequences for the well-being of the entire community, the society and the planet itself. So, too, we must enable students to understand how significant a factor gender is in the organization of economies.

Today economic exploitation of women and other unjust conditions still exist. Many of them are addressed by development programmes, but others are the causes of conflicts within and between nations. Promoting understanding of these conflicts and how to prevent them from becoming violent is one of the tasks addressed by peace education. Educating for economic capacities in a globalized economy, however, is a more difficult task because most people have little sense of connection to the global economy and do not understand their place in it. Those who educate for a culture of peace face a great challenge in this regard. They must try to help learners to understand the world economy and how to work towards its becoming both fair and productive as they provide for their own and their communities' economic needs. This must be one of the peace components of development education and of the economic training of all citizens, including those in business schools.

At the most basic level, education for the development of constructive economic capacities, therefore, should enable learners to understand their own local and national economies and the interrelations between them. And it should equip them with skills to provide a standard of living that enables the citizen and her/his family to live in health with dignity. When the economic structures and conditions appear unable to provide opportunities for wellbeing and dignity on a gender-equal basis, the responsibility of education to capacitate learners to diagnose the economic obstacles and contribute to their elimination becomes even greater. Educators need to be aware of the economic possibilities and problems that will face the learners they are preparing to function as economically productive citizens, committed to the achievement of an economically just society. Economic justice and gender justice are hallmarks of a culture of peace, and they are closely interrelated issues. Learners need to be equipped to help achieve these hallmarks and resolve the issues.

Understanding the realities of global economics and its gendered aspects becomes more and more important to the capacity to function as a global citizen. Citizen education for a culture of peace should include study of world economic and monetary institutions and policies and the international agreements that have created them. Understanding that economic policies and structures have gender consequences is essential to economic justice. The United Nations Development Programme takes this fact into account in its annual *Human Development Report* which regularly includes a gender analysis of the substance of the report. It is becoming more evident that economic capacities are necessary to fulfil personal, political and social responsibilities. As will be explained below, these capacities are the attributes that can be elicited and refined into the skills that inform the key instructional objectives of peace education. Capacities are generated from within the learner. Skills are developed and built into behavioural repertoires through the practical modes of instruction which comprise a significant component of the field of peace education.

• Care and hope: the essentials of peace

The two most essential capacities of all those that will facilitate the emergence of a culture of peace are care and hope. Without the capacity to care for the Earth, to care for others and for future generations such a culture can never come to be. For above all a culture of peace would be a culture of caring. Caring in the present culture is perhaps the most gendered capacity, for it is almost exclusively confined to the feminine sphere. While most of it is done in the private realm of home and family, even in the public realm of social services to the poor, the elderly, children and the sick, the work of care is done primarily by women. With the exception of breast-feeding, there is no biological reason for this 'division of labour'. It is the consequence of cultural practice and social organization.

The arts and skills of caring are learned. It is a human capacity that lies within men as well as women. We have many examples of men who are caring, and an increasing number of men are involved in care work. Care is a capacity that can be developed in everyone. If we are to develop a caring culture, all must develop this capacity to the extent of which each is capable. Care must become as important a factor in the public realm as in the private. Care is learned through practising the skills of caring. It must be practised by men as well women in the making of public policy. For all to learn to care, caring needs to be included in education, and certainly must be a major practice in education for a culture of peace in a gender perspective.

Hope, that which enables us to believe in the possibility of positive change, is the capacity that sustains human beings through the long and arduous struggles they must continually wage to realize their humanity and to humanize society. Hope, like care, is a very abstract capacity. But unlike care, it is not a gendered one. Both men and women have always given and sustained hope. Even though history has overlooked most of those women who have given great hope to the world, we know they have always been there. Such people have sometimes been called visionaries. Hope is the capacity out of which men and women can form the working partnerships so essential to envisioning and realizing a culture of peace. Hope can be elicited and developed through practising the skills of visioning, imaging and modelling.

Foundational concepts

Attributes

Attributes are essential characteristics of persons and communities, those elements of personality and community identity, the values, capacities and abilities which define persons, influence how they relate to and are perceived by others. Attributes are also subject to development and refinement through education. Among the goals of education for a culture of peace in a gender perspective is the development of persons who bear the attributes of peacefulness and gender sensitivity.

Capacities

Capacities are human attributes and abilities that can be developed through the experiences and learning that constitute education. The Latin verb from which the English word education derives is 'educare' meaning to lead forth, that is, to elicit. Teaching is intended to elicit these capacities, to develop them to serve socially constructive purposes. See 'Excellence in Education through

Peacemaking' [13] for a description of peace-making capacities asserted to be primary objectives of peace education. Discuss how the capacities described in the article extend and complement those described in this section as you determine other capacities or extend and deepen the concepts posed in the two texts.

• Citizenship

To be a citizen gives an individual standing in a nation-state which carries legal rights and responsibilities within the state. 'Citizen' also connotes being a part of a civil society in which persons also have rights and responsibilities that are social and ethical in nature. It is the fulfilment of these social and ethical rights and responsibilities that most concerns education for a culture of peace, as it is from the realm of civil society that the aspirations and actions for the transformation of the culture of war and violence and the achievement of gender justice are arising.

• Human diversity

Cultural diversity is complemented and extended by human diversity, which refers to the differences and varieties that characterize individual persons, as well cultures, social systems, economic systems, political systems, and ecosystems. Harmoniously functioning diversity makes for stronger, more resilient systems. Diversity is seen as essential to a resilient and sustainable environment and a viable global culture of peace. Human diversity offers a broad range of capacities for the resolution of problems and the building of a positive future.

• System

Systems are interrelated component parts, functioning together to accomplish a purpose. Systems are healthy when all the component parts function well and the authentic purpose is being achieved. When this is not the case, systems can and have been changed. The war system is intended to provide for the security of nations and their peoples. However, war and preparation for war have so endangered the health and safety of the human family; they undermine the very purpose they purport to serve. Since war has strongly affected the political and economic systems of the world it must be addressed when educating for the development of economic and political capacities.

• Declaration

A declaration is a statement of principles, values and aspirations to explain what those who have drafted it hope to achieve and why they are devising particular policies and undertaking certain actions. Declarations have preceded significant historical changes. They are issued by the United Nations from conferences and the General Assembly. Declarations have often preceded the drafting and enactment of the conventions that established, for instance, the international human-rights standards. A declaration committed the Member States of UNESCO to undertake peace education. A declaration of the General Assembly validated a culture of peace as a common goal of the international organization. The students of the International Schools put forth their vision of the education they need in a draft declaration, and the body of all the international human rights treaties rests upon the Universal Declaration of Human Rights.

• Holism

This is the practice of looking at matters of concern or a problem area as a whole; that is, to take into account all the component parts and issues concerned, observing their interrelations and how changes, interventions, or any action affecting one part affects the relationships, the other parts and the whole. Peace education uses both analytic (focus on the discrete parts) and holistic (focus on the whole) approaches.

- ## Non-violence

This term applies to the philosophy, theory and practice of conducting political or social campaigns and struggles or conflicts without inflicting harm on opponents and adversaries. Peace education advocates that the philosophical and theoretical aspects of non-violence be included as essential content. In this study unit, however, the emphasis is on the need to develop as broadly as possible a repertoire of the skills of non-violence.

- ## Tolerance

The capacity to encounter difference with respect and open-mindedness is characteristic of a tolerant person. Tolerance has also been defined as 'the acknowledgement of others' rights to life and dignity' (*Tolerance*, Unit 1, p. 54). Definitions of this and all the terms listed below are presented and discussed in *Tolerance – The Threshold of Peace*. As you reflect on them, think of how each concept may be affected by gender and how each relates to a culture of peace.

- ## Ethnocentrism

Ethnocentrism is defined in *Tolerance* (Unit 1, p. 29) as 'exclusion on the basis of culture or language: rationalized by the notion of different levels of value and "advancement" among cultures'. This definition appears in a list of indicators of severe forms of intolerance. In general, it refers to belief in the superiority of one's own culture, and the lack of capacity to appreciate or understand other cultures. More research is needed in order to provide a gendered understanding of ethnicity.

- ## Racism

Tolerance (Unit 1, p. 29) defines racism as 'the denial of human rights on the basis of race; rationalized by the assertion that some racial groups are superior to others'. Many believe that racism, defined as the belief in superior and inferior races, was elaborated as a rationale for the exploitation and domination of one group by another.

• Sexism

This form of intolerance is defined in *Tolerance* (Unit 1, p. 29) as 'Policies and behaviours that exclude women from full participation in society: rationalized by the assumption that men are intrinsically superior to women'. Sexism is a belief that pervades and maintains patriarchy, the system of male domination.

• Xenophobia

'Fear and dislike of foreigners and those of other cultures; belief that "outsiders" will harm society' is the definition offered in *Tolerance* (Unit 1, p. 29). Xenophobia has heightened ethnic tensions and ignited violence in areas of the world characterized by rapid demographic change such as an influx of foreign workers or refugees.

• Learning processes and projects

• Processes

Perspective taking with a focus on gender

Learning to look at the world and the challenges that it presents from multiple perspectives is an objective of education for tolerance, diversity and complexity. The following exercises offer an approach to taking the perspectives of others: world regions, cultures, religions and genders. Instructors may have to assign background reading if students do not have knowledge of other world regions and cultures.

1. Form teams of four to write and role-play scenarios for situations dealing with some of the following issues:
    - Relationship capacities: receiving an appeal to action on behalf of or provide humanitarian assistance to unknown people in a far distant, remote area.
    - Appreciation of diversity: an encounter with a recent immigrant unfamiliar with the culture of your country.
    - Moral inclusion: a case of gender discrimination.
    - Political capacities: repealing an unjust law.
    - Economic capacities: taking a job in an industry responsible for severe environmental damage.
    - Other situations within the realms of the various human capacities discussed here might be substituted or added.

2. Each group writes a brief scenario with four parts, each representing a perspective based on gender, combined with ethnicity, prosperous class or country, poor class or country, different religious and or cultural traditions.

3. Role-play the scenario for the class, acting as you believe the perspective of your role would lead you to do.

4. Ask the class to comment on the scenario and the role-playing, noting how the perspectives portrayed are different from the ones they would have taken and observing the levels of development of the human capacities for peace that were demonstrated. Make special note of attitudes towards gender that were depicted. Was there evidence of gender bias, gender blindness, or gender awareness and sensitivity?

5. Role-players comment on what insights they may have gained from trying to take another perspective. Did the viewers and/or the role-players learn anything about gender as a factor or the perspective of the other gender? How would they apply these learnings to their own teaching?

Human capacities to be developed in education for a culture of peace

Variations

The same scenarios could be played assigning different roles, changing the cultures and world regions referred to, and/or by assigning the scenarios written by the groups to other groups.

This or similar exercises should be repeated to offer all class members opportunities to view issues and problems from various perspectives and to gain an appreciation of how taking multiple perspectives deepens understanding of others as well as comprehension of issues and problems. Negotiation of a conflict-resolution case can also be used as a basis of exercises in perspective-taking.

• Projects

Choose one of the capacities and develop some learning strategies and lesson plans to help the students you will be teaching develop that capacity. Keep in mind as you do so that gender differences and gender equality must be considered, and that the capacity should be applied to the achievement of a culture of peace. Devise some teaching units to teach caring skills to both boys and girls.

Suggested readings

- **Learning, The Treasure Within, The Report of the International Commission on Education for the 21st Century**, Paris, UNESCO, 1995
- **Bringing CEDAW Home: The Shadow Reports**, New York, UNIFEM, 1998.
- **Nell Noddings, Caring: A Feminist Approach to Ethics and Moral Education**, Berkeley, University of California Press, reprint edit., March 1986.

Recommended research

Contact the United Nations Division for the Advancement for Women to request a list of Shadow Reports. Request copies of those that may have been filed by organizations in your country or in countries in which you have special interest. Request also the governmental reports filed by these same countries.

Identify the issues raised and the perspectives taken by the reports and compare the governmental reports to the non-governmental Shadow Reports. Prepare a model policy statement to present to the government to argue for the implementation of the concerns outlined in the Shadow Reports. These reports deal with the advancement of women through the fulfilment of CEDAW and Beijing Platform for Action obligations. What other policy recommendations would you make to assure gender equality in the issue areas addressed in the reports? How should men be involved in the changes called for?

Section 4
Social skills: learning to act with others for socially constructive purposes

Preparatory readings

- **World Declaration on Education for All: Meeting Basic Learning Needs** and **Framework for Action: Meeting Basic Learning Needs** (World Conference on Education for All, Jomtien, Thailand, 5–9 March 1990) [16]. URL: http://www.unesco.org/education/efa/ed_for_all/background/background_documents.shtml.

- **The Dakar Framework for Action – Education for All: Meeting our Collective Commitments** (World Education Forum, Dakar, Senegal, 26–28 April 2000) [17]. URL: http://www.unesco.org/education/efa/wef_2000/index.shtml.

  Both of these documents may also be ordered from UNESCO, EFA Secretariat, 7, place de Fontenoy, 75352 Paris 07 SP, France, and UNICEF, United Nations Plaza, New York, NY 10017, USA [16].

- **Ingeborg Breines, Robert Connell and Ingrid Eide (eds.), Male Roles, Masculinities and Violence: A Culture of Peace Perspective**, Paris, UNESCO Publishing, 2000.

• Socialization: context for skills development

In contemplating the learning climate in which skills are developed from a peace and gender perspective, two factors must be kept in mind; skills, as noted in the case of care, are often developed for the performance of gender roles, and in many cultures skills are valued most when they contribute to the capacity to compete. As competition is seen to be played out more in the public realm traditionally populated by men, skills development in boys is seen as preparation for competition. Care and co-operation, perceived as attributes of the private realm of family and close community are seen as skills essential to girls. Thus boys have traditionally been educated for public economic and political roles. Girls in most cultures are still educated for caring and domesticity, roles that have long kept them from enjoying equal educational opportunities, and thus denied them political, economic and social equality.

There is good reason to believe that boys can learn co-operation as they already do in the athletic teams in which they compete against other teams. Girls can also be competitive as seen in spelling bees, other children's games, and more and more in sports. Both sexes have the capacities for care and co-operation, and for competition, but education has not helped them to develop these capacities equally. Thus it is that girls are still perceived to be 'naturally' co-operative and boys 'innately' competitive. Here is a case where gender awareness is crucial to bringing about educational practices that provide equal educational opportunities for girls and boys.

It is of utmost importance that education for a culture of peace in a gender perspective be developed so as to provide equal opportunity and to increase the capacities of all to co-operate for the common good and to compete constructively in the struggle to devise and select more humane and mutually enhancing social roles and institutions.

• Skills of co-operation

Human capacities are realized through the skills with which they are manifested. Those capacities out of which a culture of peace will be drawn will manifest through a set of skills which are, in essence, life skills of persons prepared to live in a culture of peace.

These are the social skills through which the transformations called for in the United Nations Declaration and Programme of Action on a Culture of Peace can be realized. Education of the whole person for a culture of peace must include such general life skills cast in the frame of a peaceful social order. Three essential sets of skills for life in a culture of peace are: communication skills, intercultural interaction, and conflict processing skills.

Human capacities evolve and develop in association and interaction with others. All human associations are affected by personal values, interpersonal and intergroup relationships and ability to take political and economic responsibility. The levels of capacity development depend in part on the skill with which persons enter into association with others and conduct their interactions. The fundamental bases of these associations in the context of culture of peace are the very ethical principles and human values designated as the core of a peace curriculum. The development of these values and peace-related human capacities is cultivated more through the atmosphere and relationships in the classroom than by the content of the curriculum. Skill development, however, requires explicit instruction and practice. The quality of social life for any group is a consequence of the skill with which the members conduct their day-to-day interactions. Instruction in and practice of social skills should thus be a daily part of all education. This is an area in which peace education is carried out through carefully planned, specifically sequenced instruction. To prepare for this aspect of their teaching, teachers themselves must practise these skills. They need also to develop techniques to teach how to undertake co-operative endeavours, to engender a spirit of co-operation and community in the classroom.

For some teachers this responsibility may mean resisting the competitive ethos which prevails in so many schools, alienating students from each other, a preparation for the competitive world of a culture of war and violence. Academic competition can contribute to tensions between genders, ethnic or racial groups, athletes and studious students and any number of various other human differences which can be found among members of a class or school. Competitive classrooms frequently set up hierarchies of worth and social importance within the school, replicating the society's social inequities that produce conflicts. Such conditions are antithetical to democratic classrooms and to the development of a community of learners, all of whom might benefit from the differences between them. When differences are used in the learning process as a source of multiple approaches to the common learning tasks, students not only learn to respect differences, but also to use them for socially constructive purposes. They can be taught to see all human differences, including gender, as potential points of complementarity through which the whole community is enriched and strengthened.

The use of differences in interests, learning styles and ways of thinking as complementary resources to enhance the learning of all provides students with the positive experiences with difference that would characterize a culture of peace. Co-operative learning techniques are the basis of a pedagogy intended to provide such experience. Teachers should develop ways to structure learning sequences and processes so as to enable students to work together in collaborative endeavours to acquire information, analyse issues, draw conclusions and solve problems. Communities populated by persons equipped with a range of well-honed co-operative skills are likely to be communities that can clarify controversies, solve problems and resolve conflicts in creative and constructive ways. The most effective way to mainstream peace in education is the introduction of co-operative learning.

Participatory and co-operative forms of pedagogy in which students actively participate in task groups are most effective in achieving the social purposes and the learning objectives of education for a culture of peace. Learning how to identify tasks and their component parts, determining what skills and capacities are needed to undertake them, assessing the human and other resources available to the task group, formulating a plan and schedule through which the resources can be applied to the task and devising means to assess the results are components of a process through which a group can achieve a common goal. This or similar processes are the means for conducting a democratic process of change, be it learning in the classroom where students grow and change as persons and citizens, or in larger communities where citizens undertake civic and communal tasks and projects. As such these processes like those of discussion must be conducted so as to contribute to the mainstreaming of peace and gender. They must observe principles of equality, democracy and gender sensitivity.

Using projects as a teaching methodology, combined with elements of co-operative learning where students share their talents and efforts so as to increase the overall learning of all group members, is very well suited to the development of the social skills necessary for the fulfilment of civic responsibility and functioning as a constructive member of the community in which one lives and the larger communities to which these local communities are related. Projects are most appropriate for education for active participation in a global civil society.

Other areas in which these skills can be honed are student organizations, community service and co-operative learning programmes in which schools co-operate with other institutions to provide learning experiences not available within the schools. Apprenticeship programmes and volunteer service are among the educational innovations that can help the school itself to benefit from co-operative learning while providing active, experiential learning for students. Experiential learning of this kind is especially relevant when the experiences are with organizations or institutions devoted to peace, the defence of human rights, protecting the environment, overcoming poverty and disease, and/or the achievement of gender justice.

• Communication skills

Co-operative forms of learning and the social skills they are intended to develop are very dependent on the most basic set of social skills, those of communication. Exchanging ideas, imparting and processing information and many social interactions depend

Social skills: learning to act with others for socially constructive purposes

upon the ability to communicate. Schools must assure that all students can use their national language or languages with ease and fluency. Where students have a mother-tongue different from the national or official languages, they should be helped to learn in their mother-tongue as they learn the additional languages. As has been noted in the UNESCO publications on tolerance, all languages should be honoured, and lack of mastery of particular tongues should not remain a barrier to the right to education. In a culture of peace, multilingualism would be a valued skill. Wherever possible all students should have opportunities to learn other languages.

Whether or not multilingualism can be developed among any group of learners, all people, as is declared in *Education for All*, have the right to know fully one language, to speak it fluently, to read it critically and to write it articulately and reflectively. Thus, in addition to skills of discussion, the basic skills of literacy should be developed to a stage where they are in fact useful tools for social interaction in various spheres, such as economic activity for the sake of self and community, and political participation for the sake of full-fledged democracy. Educators need to be aware that gender inequality in the development of these skills at any level, from the most basic to the most sophisticated, is antithetical to the core principles of equality and democracy. Male and female students should have equal and full opportunity to develop communications skills throughout the educational process from primary to further education. Fundamental language skills should be integrated into all levels of schooling so that all learners can continue to develop various capacities to communicate with a broad range of others.

Differences in communications styles of gender, class and ethnicity should be honoured and used as resources as other differences should be. Gender sensitivity is a communication skill that acknowledges and respects differences in communications styles between boys and girls, men and women. It acknowledges and addresses such gender difference in communication as those that lead women to believe that they are not 'listened to' by men, and men that they are not 'understood' by women, a problem also sometimes found in cross-cultural communication.

Educators should keep in mind also that well-developed communication skills include reflective listening, participatory hearing, articulate speech and the ability to clarify. Reflective listening helps to develop the capacity to listen for the meanings, values and concerns of those with whom we communicate. It requires not only a focus on what is said, but also why it is said and what the speaker feels, thinks and hopes the listener will understand. Participatory hearing is a way of expressing interest, concern and comprehension by integrating what others say into one's own contributions to a discussion. All these elements need to be understood for communication that will lead to peaceful, mutually enhancing relationships. We know that they are essential to negotiations of all kinds, most especially in peace-making.

A well-developed ability to use language is important to all relationships and social functions, and essential to peaceful relations between persons, groups and nations. When communications skills are limited, problem-solving and conflict resolution capacities are also limited. Persons who can express themselves with assurance do not fall so easily into the frustration that can produce the anger that often leads to hostility and conflict. The adage that advises to use words and negotiations instead of fists and weapons to settle differences cannot be applied if the disputants do not have the words or the communications skills with which to negotiate. The young need to be taught how to express their emotions and their thoughts in ways that respect the dignity and humanity of those with whom they differ. Education should provide opportunities to learn these skills in many forms. Care should be taken that both boys and girls are given equal opportunities to be heard and to practise all communications skills.

Educators can also cultivate means of communication other than language. The arts, the use of drawing, poetry, drama, dance and other art forms to articulate ideas and express emotions and aspirations can help to bring variety to the classroom and nurture the creative capacities that will be needed to conceptualize and

Social skills: learning to act with others for socially constructive purposes

realize a culture of peace. The arts are a major form of communication for social purposes, and as such have an important role to play in educating for a culture of peace. In the teaching techniques of drawing or drama, for example, teachers can provide opportunities to deal with the themes of peace, human rights, democracy and gender justice. All teachers can be peace educators if they intentionally pursue the goals and observe the principles of education for a culture of peace with a gender perspective.

Cultural skills

As indicated in Section 1, gender is culturally derived and contextualized. Developing an understanding of culture as the way peoples realize their humanity is a prerequisite to an authentic gender perspective. Cultural skills comprise such understanding as well as the ability to interpret events and behaviours in their respective cultural contexts. These skills are among those that will be ever more important in a multicultural peaceful world, if the future is to be one in which the cultures of all are to survive in dignity. Certainly they are necessary to the formation and implementation of policies to realize the international standards for human rights and gender equality in a manner observant of the dignity and integrity of all cultures. Students being prepared for active, responsible citizenship in a varied, often conflictual, world society need to be educated to appreciate other ways of life, to understand at least one other culture deeply through study of its belief systems, customs, ways of looking at the world, the history of its people and how the culture relates to others.

Language learning and multilingualism are important to a culture of peace as has been observed above in addressing the need to develop communication skills. It is important that language teaching for a culture of peace be directed towards a fuller understanding of another people, as well as fluency in their language. Through language, students can strive to attain as deep an understanding as they can of another people, learning as well some general concepts about all cultures, how they are formed, function and change. Languages and the cultures they express vary in the degree to which they are gendered, some manifesting different forms of speech for men and women. Study of this aspect of language can contribute to an understanding of gender formation in the culture. It is especially important that the study of other cultures include the patterns of gender formation and gender relations in the cultures being studied if a gender perspective is to be brought to bear on intercultural understanding.

• Conflict skills

Cultural differences can, but need not, lead to conflicts. Most culturally produced conflicts stem from misunderstandings and misinterpretation. As intercultural and multicultural education become more prevalent, complemented and extended by education for tolerance, such conflicts should be reduced. With a high enough level of cultural proficiency among the peoples of the earth, intercultural conflict need no longer pose so great a threat to peace. Given, however, the rate of change and the great variety of differences in perspectives that exist in world society, conflict is likely to be a part of human life well into the future. In a culture of peace, conflict would be one of the processes through which positive change takes place. It will certainly continue to be prevalent through the generation during which the world learns its way to a peace characterized by diversity and justice. Conflict-processing skills are among the most basic to be learned if people are to be able to build and maintain mutually enhancing relationships.

Conflict skills are integral to all positive relationships from the interpersonal to the international. They are basic life skills that individuals and institutions have occasions to apply on a daily basis. Conflict is a part of all our lives; yet few of us have the skills to transform conflict from a painful destructive process to one of significant learning and constructive change. As pain indicates a malfunction in the body, conflict is a symptom of a serious problem in a relationship. If left untreated these problems can lead to damaging, even permanent, ruptures in troubled relationships. Such ruptures in cases of interethnic or international conflicts often lead to devastating cycles of violence and warfare which can be lethal to entire societies. Constructive conflict processing is to troubled relationships what the healing arts and sciences are to the body. Taking an ecological or living systems approach to conflict enables us to understand it as a potentially pathological condition which can be 'healed' through therapies such as non-violent conflict resolution, adjudication by law, application of human rights standards or other such instruments designed to achieve and maintain a healthy society built on positive relationships among the members.

Conflicts must be recognized, confronted, resolved and where possible transformed into dynamic and peaceful processes of cultural, social, economic or political change. Actual and potential conflicts in all these spheres now rage, many of them very violent, many threatening to produce future wars. Leaders and citizens alike need training in conflict management, conflict transformation and conflict resolution. They need to be able to work through conflicts in such a way as to prevent them from harming the participants. Most urgently, they need to be able to avoid and prevent the armed conflicts and wars that brought such havoc to the last century and inflicted irreparable harm on the lives and communities of millions. This requires a repertoire of conflict processing skills of various types. It calls for a review and assessment of the various approaches taken to conflict by different cultures, as well as consideration of gender differences in conflict processing. Scholars and researchers in the field of conflict resolution have made note of distinctly different styles often used by men and women. Study of traditional modes of conflict processing and resolution used by some ethnic and indigenous groups should be included in the conflict skills repertoire as well as the practices devised by professionals in the field.

The UNESCO document [26] referred to in Section 8 on teaching approaches outlines African process approach to conflict.

It is one model of how to provide students with learning opportunities to enable them to deal constructively with conflict at various stages of a conflict process. Processes are not inexorable. Negative ones can be interrupted, aborted and prevented. Positive ones can be initiated, encouraged and completed. And, most hopefully, negative processes can be transformed into positive processes as is the case with conflict transformation.

Foundational concepts

Reflective listening/participatory hearing

This refers to the essential need to listen with full attention to all speakers if a discussion group is to provide learning for all participants. Emphasis is on both listening and hearing to indicate that what we hear is not so much what is said as how we interpret it. Participatory, interpretive hearing connotes the essential need of listeners to seek clarity from speakers. This need applies to all discussions and is especially acute in peace-related discussion and conflict resolution.

Skills

Skills as used in this study unit means the procedural and technical abilities to perform tasks directed to social goals and instructional tasks and to train others to perform procedures for achieving objectives such as analysing a problem or resolving a conflict. Skills are acquired through instruction and perfected through practice and reflection on the results of the practice, enabling the learner to perfect the skill by improving practice.

Repertoire

Repertoire is a term borrowed from the performing arts, but as an educational term it refers to a range of skills at a person's command. A repertoire is built through repeated practice of various skills, thus emphasizing the importance of practical and experiential learning and of multiple action possibilities to peace education.

• Conflict resolution

While conflict resolution is one function of non-violence, it is only one. So, too, there are aspects of the practice of conflict resolution that are not generally considered in the realm of non-violence; and, as will be observed in the section on teaching approaches, resolution is but one stage of the entire process of conflict.

• Learning processes and projects

• Processes

Reflective listening/participatory hearing

Instructors should emphasize that good communication is a co-operative endeavour, and observe that nothing validates a person's sense of dignity and worth so much as 'being heard' or 'attended to'. As noted in the text, this sense and the skill that produces it are very important to clear and open communication, especially between women and men, and between individuals of different cultures, and most crucially in peace-making processes. The following exercises are instructional devices to facilitate listening/hearing skills. Here 'listening' refers to 'attending' or paying attention, and 'hearing' to 'interpreting' and understanding.

1. Ask the students to pair off in teams of two. Begin with teams of the same sex as much as possible. Each team is to discuss one of the topics on the following list, according to the set of rules outlined below the list:

Topics
- Co-operative learning as a means to intercultural understanding.
- Gender sensitivity as a facilitator of communication.
- Conflict resolution as a fundamental life skill.

Rules
- Each member of the team takes two to three minutes to express an opinion and give reasons for holding it; during the speaking turn of one partner the other listens in attentive silence, focusing intently on what is being said and simultaneously (and silently) interpreting what is being meant.
- At the end of the three minutes the listener tells the speaker what she/he believed was said and meant, that is, restates the opinion expressed and the reasons for it.
- The first speaker indicates that the listener interpreted correctly or clarifies if necessary, without interruptions, any misinterpretations that she/he perceives.
- The other team member takes two to three minutes to express an opinion and give reasons.
- The partner listens attentively, silently and then restates what she/he perceived to be the opinion and reasons of the second speaker.
- The second speaker responds uninterrupted as did the first speaker.
- No interruptions or verbal responses while one partner is speaking are allowed during this exchange. Also avoid judgmental facial expressions and body language.
- When completed the partners may freely discuss the exchange and express their reactions to being listened to and heard.

2. Try the same exercise with mixed-gender teams, assigning each a different one of the three topics.

3. Discuss the two rounds asking for first reactions to being listened to and being heard and then noting whether differences

Social skills: learning to act with others for socially constructive purposes

were perceived between the single-gender groups and the mixed-gender groups. Ask what might account for these differences and what can be learned towards improving communication between genders.

4. Form groups of five to seven students to discuss the importance of skills-teaching and learning techniques to facilitate skills development. Each group is to be conducted according to the following procedure:

   • Select a discussion facilitator and a reporter who will not participate in the discussion.

   • Each of the participants is to take one to two minutes to set forth an opinion uninterrupted and be attentively listened to by all other discussants, facilitator and reporter.

   • Next, each participant gets a chance to add to one of the statements of the others, integrating that statement into this intervention to indicate that it has been heard. These statements are also to be uninterrupted. This round may then be followed by a more free-flowing discussion, guided by the facilitator so that all are heard, and points are clarified.

   • The reporter then gives the group an assessment of the level of attention and the accuracy of interpretation, and the group will help to clarify the report before it is presented to the class.

5. After the reports, ask the students to assess where they need to improve their communication skills and enter into their journals a plan to achieve the improvement with notes on how they will use these skills in their teaching and how they will help their own students to develop them.

6. As these skills are further developed, students should be guided in learning how to constructively challenge a position or opinion of another, how to identify and build upon points of complementarity, clarify differences, develop consensus and accept and articulate divergent and alternative positions.

• Projects

Compare the skills described in this section with those advocated in *Global Citizenship: A Draft Declaration* [12].

Develop a set of teaching units to teach skills of co-operation working together on a common task, using the particular knowledge and talents of all on the co-operating team; and another set for 'positive competition' in which winning is helping others most effectively to achieve their goals or helping to devise the most constructive way to achieve a common goal.

Arrange a set of co-operative projects and/or community action endeavours with local service organizations, peace groups and/or women's groups.

Suggested readings

- **David Johnson, Roger Johnson and Karl Smith,** *Co-operative Learning: Increasing College Faculty Instructional Productivity*, Washington, D.C., George Washington University, 1991.
- **G. Pike and D. Selby,** *Global Teacher, Global Learner*, London, Hodder & Staughton, 1988.
- **Sanaa Osseiran,** *Handbook Resource and Teaching Material in Conflict Resolution, Education for Human Rights, Peace and Democracy*, Paris, IPRA, with the support of UNESCO, 1994.
- **R. W. Connell**, Teaching the Boys: New Research on Masculinity, and Gender Strategies for Schools, *Teachers College Record*, Vol. 98, No. 2, Winter 1996.
- **Miriam Miedzian,** *Boys Will Be Boys: Breaking the Link Between Masculinity and Violence*, New York, Anchor Books, 1992.

Recommended research

Review the literature of teaching skills development in your country. Prepare a bibliography. Each student picks one title, reads and reviews the work, assessing its relevance to the social needs presented by the go of educating for a culture of peace and gender equality. Share the reviews in class.

Review the literature on gender socialization and schooling. Select som readings and form discussion groups to report on findings on gender socialization and schooling.

Section 5

Global problems as obstacles
to a culture of peace

Preparatory readings

- **Excerpts from the Beijing Platform for Action from the fourth World Conference on Women** [14].
- **Declaration on the Elimination of Violence against Women**, United Nations General Assembly Resolution 48/104, 20 December 1993.
- **A Declaration of Human Rights from a Gender Perspective**, 22 January 1998 (UN DOC. E/CN.4/1998/NGO/3).
- **Hans Kung, Universal Declaration of Human Responsibility**, the Interaction Commission, 1997, interact@asiawide.or.jp.

• Violence and gender: tools for assessing global problems

The content of peace education, from whatever perspective it is approached, must provide knowledge and understanding of what must be undone as well as what must be done in the process of global transformation. Learners must be guided towards a clear comprehension of the major obstacles to a culture of peace: the normative and behavioural obstacles that lie at the heart of our discussion of capacities and skills; and the institutional and existential obstacles, the global problems that are worldwide manifestations of the culture of war. Together these problems comprise the problematic of creating a culture of peace. What follows is a very brief overview of some of those problems in light of the growing evidence of gender and violence as central factors in this set of interrelated problems. All are the foci of extensive research and the subjects of bodies of literature that can be of great use to educators seeking to prepare teachers to make schools an instrument of a culture of peace.

Violence and gender injustice lie at the heart of the problematic. All our current global problems are the consequence or manifestation of some form of violence. One way of looking at the main tasks of creating a culture of peace is to think of the primary goals as reducing and eliminating violence, and enhancing and universalizing human dignity and equality by increasing gender justice. Every global problem also has a gender dimension, the recognition of which is integral to its resolution in the present and essential to its longer-term transformation. Coming to understand this fact has led the United Nations to focus on its gender mainstreaming policy, and the organization's advocacy of such a policy to Member States. The actual advocacy within Member States has been conducted mainly by women's organizations and feminists, largely because it is women who bear the major burden of the world's gender imbalance in power and the gender injustice that prevails in most societies. These conditions and the advocacy movements to overcome them have led to many changes in international and national policies. They have also produced an extensive literature on women's roles in and perspectives on international relations and peace-making [18].

Women's perspectives are, of course, only half of a full gender perspective. However, given the disadvantages women bear in a world society that has yet to give adequate attention to gender, and the fact that most 'gender neutral' policy is based on a presumption of male as ordinary or 'normal', women's perspectives are a good starting point to work towards gender balance and gender justice. We will note here some of the highlights of women's relationships to the major forms of violence that comprise four crucial, core global problems: environmental deterioration, poverty and mal-development, violations of human rights and social injustice, war and various forms of systematic physical violence. We will also observe some aspects of the problems as they relate to men, so that those following this syllabus will have the beginnings of a full gender perspective as the basis for a broader consideration of gender and as a background from which to bring a gender perspective to their own efforts to educate for a culture of peace. To do so, we need to keep ever in our minds these two crucial dimensions of peace education – violence and gender.

Violence, as we have noted, is avoidable and intentional harm inflicted in the pursuit of goals or purposes sought by particular individuals or groups, without regard to the rights or needs of others. Thus, we have the fundamental principle to guide the most essential learnings for transformation of a culture of war into a culture of peace – non-violence. We must learn first and foremost a range of tactics and strategies for avoiding harm in the transformation of cultures, most of which assume that violence is sometimes (in recent history often) necessary. We must ask ourselves: 'What are other non-harmful and, when possible, mutually beneficial ways in which to confront the issues and problems that tend to produce violence?' This is a prime instance in which learning to envision and design alternatives becomes a major educational objective.

The transitional nature of this task also calls for developing a capacity to make distinctions, such as that between sex and gender. Two other crucial distinctions to be made are those between intentional and unintentional harm, and between destructive violence and legitimate force. While we speak of violent storms and perhaps violent spasms of the body and the like, these destructive processes are not the result of human intent. Societies try to find ways to avoid suffering and destruction of all kinds, and plan ways to repair and restore what is damaged in such cases. Indeed, a culture of peace would permit human societies to devote more attention and resources to these kinds of efforts. What education for peace must undertake is the facilitation of the learning that will enable people to understand that war and the other forms of physical, economic, political, ecological and gender violence are not of the same order as natural disasters. These are not inevitable eventualities to be prepared for; these are the consequences of human will and intent and can be avoided, even eliminated entirely if human will and intent so determine. We can prepare for peace as intentionally and systematically as we prepare for potential 'natural disasters'. Education, particularly learning about alternatives to violence, is the major component of that preparation.

The fact that destructive processes and behaviours, while not all inevitable, are likely to be part of human life for some time to come, makes the distinction between violence and legitimate force an even more important issue for peace education. Peace-keeping, as the concept was originally derived, was conceived as legitimate force. Legitimate force is physical, sometimes armed, power applied under the rule of law or the consensus of the communities concerned, to halt or prevent the unfolding of a destructive process. The arrest of criminals; the restraint of persons who may do harm to themselves or others; protective restraint of dangerous behaviour on the part of children unaware of the consequences of their actions; and teachers using their authority to stop unruly or otherwise destructive behaviour are all forms of legitimate force.

Such force can and has become violent. Even peacekeepers have sometimes resorted to armed force prematurely or without sufficient cause. What we know as police brutality are incidents in which agents of legitimate force have caused avoidable or intentional harm, harm not necessary for achieving their legitimate purpose. It is the assessment of these two aspects, necessity and intentionality, that has been used to determine whether police and law-enforcement officers have committed violent acts. These are two elements we have to learn to fit into our assessment of what constitutes the kinds of violent behaviours, policies and institutions that a culture of peace would seek to transform. They can also be useful criteria in determining what aspects of gender call for change.

Gender is an extremely useful lens through which to examine global problems, because, being culturally derived and socially constructed, gender roles and relations are the consequence of human intent and, as has been demonstrated, subject to change. As we have learned over the years since International Women's Year in 1975, most of the harm that results from gender roles is avoidable, and can, therefore, be considered violence. Although gender constructions vary from culture to culture, gender is a universal and there are identifiable commonalties that transcend culture. Also, distinctions between gender roles are apparent at all levels of society in all human cultures. Thus, it provides a perspective from which to make both particular and general observations.

Gender analysis and violence assessments of communities, and cumulatively of global society, illuminate a comprehensive diagnosis of global problems and their interrelationships. In short, they are very useful devices for those seeking a holistic approach to education for a culture of peace. Some of the pedagogic possibilities in such analyses will be identified below as proposed content for peace education. Learners must be equipped with the skills to recognize and resolve these problems, through the application of the capacities and skills outlined in Sections 3 and 4.

• Environmental deterioration

Avoidable harm to the environment is inflicted daily by millions of people in all parts of the world. Intentional environmental harm of a much higher order for the purpose of short-term economic advantage is inflicted by a much smaller number of industrial interests. Much of this environmental damage has significant gender consequences. Men and women often have different relationships to the environment. Much damage to the environment results from the forms of development derived from the Western, techno-industrial development which becomes ever more prevalent with the process of globalization. These policies are made by male power élites, most of whom live a life in which the natural environment is obscured by advanced development. Many of the avoidable, damaging effects of these policies are experienced by women in the developing countries. This is just one of many instances in which the importance of both a global and a gender perspective and violence awareness are important to understanding the problems experienced daily at the local level where the gender disparities and avoidable harm resulting from global policies are most readily apparent.

Women in some traditional societies have had a close and continuous relationship and interdependency with the natural environment. For example, women as food-raisers have engaged in farming practices that care for the soil. They have depended on forests and wooded areas for fuel and as natural flood protection. Deforestation, the introduction of industrial practices into agriculture, monocrop production and other such consequences of 'development' have increased women's vulnerability to poverty, eroded the environment and exhausted vital resources. Women scholars and activists in these areas have developed a more life-centred approach to environmental issues which views the earth and all its component parts as one living system with subsystems, human society being one of them. This approach, known as ecofeminism, also observes the similarities that exist in the abuse and exploitation of the Earth and the abuse and exploitation of women.

Gender has also played a role in the development of environmental awareness. Women because of their gender roles as care-givers were aroused earlier to the health effects of air pollution, nuclear testing and the use of poisonous substances in agriculture. The environmental movement is also one in which women have been recognized for their leadership roles. This leadership is recognized in the Beijing Platform for Action agreed upon at the fourth World Conference on Women in 1995 (Critical Area of Concern K [14]). Both men and women have equal stakes in the restoration of the environment and the responsible observation of principles of sustainable development. This responsibility must be shared equally by men and women, just as the implementation of the Beijing Platform for Action will depend upon a strong working partnership between women and men.

• Poverty and maldevelopment

Some ecological problems have resulted from poverty. There is a cycle of interdependence between poverty and environmental damage. Poverty sometimes leads to the depletion of resources such as that which results from meeting short-term fuel needs, and a depleted environment offers no basis for the development of a longer-range economic self-sufficiency. The situation seems to be on a constant downward spiral with the same constant gender imbalance. Women comprise about half the world's population, but account for 70 per cent of the world's poor. Women, too, are among the most exploited in the labour force.

Much of the human poverty that causes untold human suffering is avoidable harm. It results from inequities in the distribution of resources and benefits, and the policies that favour development of infrastructure and military expenditures over expenditures that more directly meet human needs. It persists because the structures and the decision-makers do not welcome the participation of women or the poor in making plans and setting priorities. Exclusion of the poor from economic decision-making results in the avoidable harm peace researchers call 'structural violence'.

The rapid development of 'globalization', wherein northern-based transnational corporations can more easily transcend boundaries in production and trade, has thus far tended to benefit the richer nations of the North, leaving the poorer South even further behind in its struggle against ever worsening poverty. As noted in the Beijing Platform's Area of Concern A [14], gender roles impose the greatest burden of the negative consequences of this process on women. Women also bear more of the burden in rural areas because men continue to migrate to cities seeking paid employment. So, too, 'structural adjustments' are also felt more painfully by women, because the gendered division of labour assigns household maintenance and care of family to them. Lack of paid employment prevents men from performing their gender role of income providers. Thus both men and women, while suffering

Global problems as obstacles to a culture of peace

in different ways, experience the negative consequences of maldevelopment. Understanding the differences, however, is crucial to devising effective strategies to reduce and eliminate poverty.

Human-rights violations and social injustice

Some view poverty from the perspective of human rights, seeing it as a violation of the rights enumerated in the International Convention on Economic, Social and Cultural Rights. Many struggles for economic and distributive justice have been waged in the name of human rights. The twentieth century may ultimately be known as the 'human rights century'. No other set of global issues aroused more action, and no other problems gave rise to more normative standard setting for the world community. Yet massive violations of human rights continue in all areas of the world. These violations are major causes of armed violence, exacerbating such other forms of violence as the physical violence of torture, the political violence of repression, the social violence of racism and sexism, and the most horrendous of crimes against humanity – genocide.

The international community has designated three major global problems as crimes against humanity, violence of such nature and proportions as wound the entire world community and debase the humanity not only of perpetrators and victims, but of the entire human family. Genocide, torture, and apartheid have been designated as crimes against humanity. In all cases there are gender elements. Both men and women suffer from and have been involved in committing these crimes and other human-rights violations. But here, too, a gender perspective reveals that both suffer in different ways as victims, and often function in different ways as perpetrators.

Many of the violations of the human rights of women are gender inspired and sexually inflicted. Rape and some forms of torture are clear examples of this reality. Rape is a sexual act, but it is a crime of violence. Biologically, it is so similar to sexual intercourse that it has been seen as a sexual crime rather than as an act of aggression, perpetrated for reasons of hostility (Susan Brownmiller, *Against Our Will: Men, Women and Rape*, New York, Bantam, 1976). A frequent motive behind rape is to degrade and injure the victim and the people with whom she or he identifies. This is why rape has become a systematic strategy of war, a means of demoralizing the enemy and of disgracing the opposing males. In this, as in many cases, women are seen as a commodity, the property of men or war booty wherein rape is allowed as a reward to the prevailing forces. When it is perceived as a crime, rape is often seen as a crime more against the community and male relatives than against the violated women.

Women under torture often experience devastating pain and injury that is sexual in nature. Men are also subject to sexual violation, but in the process they are psychologically, if not always physically, castrated or feminized, that is to say they are cast into the feminine gender role of being sexually subservient. These hard-to-face realities are important, because they help to account for the lack of guilt about rape and sexual slavery in war. The perpetrators, socialized into a sexist view of gender, see these atrocities not as violations of fundamental human dignity and integrity, but as essential extensions of women as socially subservient providers of sexual services to be used as resources deemed necessary to conducting a war and to be commandeered for military purposes.

The task for peace educators in this regard is to work towards cultivating the commitment to human rights advocated in the Integrated Framework of Action and an absolute respect for the bodily integrity of all human beings. It is the total lack of such respect that accounts for many human-rights violations, including military, sexual slavery, enforced prostitution of women and children, and conditions of work, also mainly of women and children, that amount to slavery. Slavery is that state in which one owns nothing including one's own body. Slavery in any form cannot exist in a culture of peace.

Gender has also been a human-rights issue in areas of political and legal status. Women, until the last century, were in many societies 'legal minors', that is, not responsible adults, who lived under the guardianship of fathers, husbands or brothers. It is the legacy of these conditions that keeps women in many instances in subservient status, denying them all the human rights encoded in the international standards. Denying the rights of women denies society the full benefits of the potential and actual contributions of half the world's population. So it is that the women's movements for human equality and gender justice have focused on the language of standard human rights. Women's human-rights actions are among the most effective of global civil society. Women organized to remove the gender blinders from human rights discussions and actions brought about the Declaration on the Elimination of all Forms of Violence against Women put forth at the World Conference on Human Rights (Vienna, 1993), and adopted by the United Nations General Assembly in 1993 [19]. The rallying cry of the 1995 fourth World Conference on Women was 'Women's Rights are Human Rights!' Human rights principles are the elements that hold together all 'Twelve Areas of Critical Concern' that comprise the main substance of the Beijing Platform for Action.

A curriculum for preparing learners to work for the realization of gender justice in a culture of peace would include study of all the international human-rights declarations and treaties, especially the Convention on the Elimination of All Forms of Discrimination against Women, the Beijing Platform for Action, and the outcome documents of the Beijing +5 meeting in New York (June 2000). It would guide learners through a process of inquiry into how these standards might be used to advance the cause of gender justice, and raise the question of whether additions and revisions even beyond the Optional Protocol to CEDAW, which provides a means through which women can claim their rights under that treaty, should be considered [20].

It was just such a process pursued by the members of the Latin American and Caribbean Council for Women's Rights that produced A Declaration of Human Rights in a Gender Perspective [21]. This declaration is to the arena of human rights what the Global Action to Prevent War (c/o World Order Models Project, 777 United Nations Plaza, New York, NY 10017) is to the arena of peace. In other words, it is a serious, well-researched proposal for steps to a more just and less violent world order put forth by responsible global citizens. It suggests new areas of rights consistent with the global problematic offered here as the core content of curricula on obstacles to a culture of peace.

Another such effort demonstrates the integral relationships between human rights and responsibilities. Clearly the violence of human rights abuses cannot be eliminated without responsible action on the part of everyone. As all are the subject of rights, all are also responsible for the protection and implementation of rights and for the wellbeing of Earth and the human community. The Inter-action Council, an international organization of former presidents and prime ministers, submitted to the United Nations in 1997 a proposed *Universal Declaration of Human Responsibilities* drafted by the ethicist philosopher and theologian Hans Kung [22].

• War and multiple forms of physical violence

War is not only the most highly organized form of violence, it is also the most systematically executed, involving virtually all other forms of physical violence. Until the Second World War (1939–45) most of the violence suffered in modern warfare took place on the battlefield, and civilian populations were not major targets of military action. During the second half of the twentieth century, in spite of international agreements to control the destructiveness and savagery of war, the balance shifted and civilian casualties now largely outnumber the military. This shift took place both as a consequence of the development of more sophisticated weapons and other, more significant changes to internal and exceedingly vicious civil wars. So, too, there has been a shift in the gender balance in bearing the costs of war. While men continue to be the majority in the armed forces, women's numbers are higher in the displaced, the homeless and the destitute who fill a proliferation of refugee camps established in the wake of numerous armed conflicts. Women also outnumber men as victims of war crimes, a fact made painfully evident when rape was acknowledged and prosecuted as such a crime. While both men and women serve in armed forces, and both men and women of all ages are among the civilian victims of war, there is an imbalance in the suffering of noncombatants weighted heavily on the side of female casualties.

Understanding these significant shifts, women peace activists argue, is essential to a gender perspective on war as a global problem. These changes in the conduct of war produced the worldwide concern that led the fourth World Conference on Women to include Women and Armed Conflict among the twelve areas of critical concern addressed by the Platform for Action [14]. Combined with the need to call attention to women's many contributions to peace-making, the need for inclusion of both women and men for a balanced gender perspective in peace processes, the changes have also led to the emergence of a growing literature on women and peace [18].

The increasing destructiveness and the wanton human suffering that are the hallmarks of war have produced not only movements of protests against a particular war, but have, even more significantly, made the cause of the abolition of war appear to be more of a practical necessity than a utopian idea. It has been recognized that the institution of war, the core of the war system and the centre of the web of competitive and adversarial relationships that comprise the culture of war and violence, is, as are all other cultural institutions, a human invention. It is a product of the human imagination and the human imagination can replace it. The world seems to be learning the fundamental truth that is UNESCO's cornerstone, that which led the agency to launch the concept that has become a major world movement, a global effort that has captured the human imagination in all cultures, a culture of peace. 'Since wars begin in the minds of men, it is in the minds of men that the defences of peace must be constructed' (Preamble to the Constitution of UNESCO, 1945).

Clearly, the abolition of war more than any other task of constructing the foundations of peace requires the disciplined development of the human imagination and creativity. Imagination complemented by rigorous research, as we have noted, has led to the formulation and projection of various alternatives to war. Educators can help to inspire the imaginations of their students by introducing them to such proposals, and by encouraging them to apply their own imaginations to the task of designing and bringing into being new institutions which would make war unnecessary and obsolete (see [8]).

Most of the work of the search for alternatives to war is taking place among members of civil society rather than within governments, and much of it has been the work of women. As the development of a culture of peace requires a partnership between women and men, the devising of institutional alternatives to war requires a partnership between governments and civil society. Women's promising contributions to peace-making have been the basis of the beginning of such a partnership, through some of the collaborative endeavours of intergovernmental agencies such as UNESCO and UNIFEM. UNESCO's Special Project on Women and a Culture of Peace in Africa is an outstanding example of such collaboration. It has helped to illuminate the possibility that the above quotation from the UNESCO Constitution might hold a double truth about the origins of war. The language that appears gender exclusive by using the term 'men' in a statement commonly thought to pertain to all humans, male and female (as the word 'men' was traditionally used), may be a statement of the fact that it is, indeed, men and not women who determine if, when and how to wage war, often leaving women as the main voices for peace. Clearly, women's peace-making skills, as noted in the UNESCO Statement on Women's Contribution to a Culture of Peace [5], are a major untapped source of possibilities for ushering forth a culture of peace. This resource was the focus of the Declaration and Plan of

Action of UNESCO's Pan African Women's Conference on a Culture of Peace and Nonviolence, held in Zanzibar in 1999 [23], and the Hanoi Declaration and Asian Women's Plan of Action for a Culture of Peace and Sustainable Development of the Asian Women for a Culture of Peace Conference, held in Viet Nam in 2000 [32], and the Windhoek Declaration of 2000 [24]. The documents call for the full political empowerment of women and their equal representation in policy and decision-making on all matters of peace and security.

War has been an important factor in socializing men and women to gender roles and behaviours. Belonging, as it seems, in the public arena and requiring in previous centuries the physical prowess and muscularity that characterize male bodies, war has been men's business. Preparation to wage war has always been a significant subtext in the socialization and education of boys, while girls have been socialized to assure that the 'home front' supported the societies' 'fighting men' and to admire the traits carefully cultivated to make men fighters, such as daring, bravery and aggressiveness, extensions of the basic competitiveness (or perhaps its origins) that is still encouraged in so many schools. Now that the home is a significant part of the 'fighting front', and civil populations are targeted rather than protected in armed conflicts, these essentially sexist cultural concepts and practices are coming into question. Men and women all over the world are observing in their own societies what is described in the context of Africa by a United Nations interagency publication.

> Gender is a social construct that marks a fundamental power relation in societies, which structures and affects both the private and public life of men and women. In African societies, housework, water carrying, child-care and family health are considered women's gender responsibilities. The men are expected to concentrate on the material needs of their families, to take up leadership and decision-making positions particularly in the public sphere, and to arm themselves and fight to protect the family, the community or nation.

Such clear sets of messages and instructions on the role of women and men lead to a situation in which a vicious cycle of sexism perpetuates the differential treatment of women, the entrenchment of rigid gender roles and the division of labour. In addition, it is a contributory factor in the inaccurate interpretations that surround the term 'gender'. Often, such misinterpretation denies the existence of the prevailing hierarchy where women are subordinated (*Best Practices in Peace-building and Non-violent Conflict Resolution*, p. 6, UNESCO/UNHCR/UNDP/UNFPA/UNICEF/UNIFEM, 1997: http://www.unesco.org/cpp/wcp).

While the waging of war and the criminal acts committed in the process are the largest-scale forms of violence, war, as has been noted, is the centre of a web or continuum of violence that pervades human societies at all levels and in all world regions. While societies vary in the degrees of violent crime they experience, all societies report higher levels of cultural and social violence, much of it 'domestic violence' committed in the home or within the family. Many attribute this rise in violence to the erosion of traditional values, some to the increase in competition and frustration that impedes satisfaction in work, or lack of work; some to the breakdown of families and gender expectations, the glorification of violence in history, the media and popular culture and other such factors. Others, feminist peace researchers among them, see all the forms of violence as extensions of the patriarchal war system, and the massive violence against women in 'peace' as well as war as interrelated problems, elements of patriarchy and indicators of the underlying culture of violence that maintains it. They argue that all these various forms of violence must be addressed in any strategy to abolish war, and conversely that war cannot be abolished without eliminating these other forms of violence that keep societies functioning with a war mentality.

Advocates of the human rights of women see violence against women as a manifestation of the sexist nature of the war system. They work to mainstream a gender perspective and gender issues in all international standards and institutions such as the recently drafted statutes for an International Criminal Court, the development of which is monitored by the NGO Caucus for Gender Justice. Thus continues the kind of efforts that led to the Declaration on Violence against Women issued from the World Conference on Human Rights and approved by the United Nations General Assembly in 1993. These views were embodied in the Beijing Platform for Action in the Critical Areas of Concern on Women in Armed Conflict and Violence Against Women. So, too, they inform precedents cited in the October 2000 Resolution 1325 of the United Nations Security Council on women, peace and security. These documents, like other such international agreements and statements, comprise bases for significant curricular content for education about overcoming obstacles to a culture of peace.

• Human security: expectations of wellbeing, justice and peace

The war system has been developed and maintained to provide for the national security of the nations of the international system. Nations continue to assume that war will be a necessity and give a high priority to preparing for it, keeping the system in place. The assumption about security that underlies the thinking that maintains the system is that threats to national security come primarily from other nations or unstable or undesirable elements within the nation. Such threats, it is argued, make it necessary for nations to possess weapons and forces to assure peace by deterring or defending themselves against such threats. Some even claim that maintaining a high state of military preparedness is necessary to prevent war.

Vast resources have gone into the maintenance of this 'security system' to defend one nation's or alliance's security against perceived threats from others, who in their turn, whether they intend to threaten or not, must also make their own preparations in the spirit of competition that characterizes the culture of war. The management of 'international security' matters has been in the hands of men, most of whom have been educated in the forms of gender identification and concepts of gender roles that make masculinity synonymous with forcefulness, the capacity to control others and assert one's will to achieve one's own or the nation's goals. Women, with very few exceptions, have not taken part in this management, and those who have tend to think about security in these same masculine terms. The feminine approach that could be brought by those socialized to caring roles, that produces a different, less competitive, more co-operative view of security, has been for the most part closed out of policy-making about peace and security. Lack of gender balance in security policy is seen by many to be a very serious obstacle to achieving a culture of peace.

A growing number of men and women concerned with the prioritizing of military means to defend security have asserted that the emphasis on militarized security stands in the way of providing adequate resources to meet human needs; that in the most fundamental sense, the human family is less secure because of the way nations choose to define and maintain 'national security'. They have begun to call for new thinking in the name of 'human security'. One particular, international group of women have been collaborating on an effort to redefine security and to find ways to stem the tide of militarization and thereby increase the security of the whole human family. They argue that we need to think of security in the comprehensive, holistic terms that peace education has advocated as the most effective approach to problem-solving in a global and diverse society. They are developing a security inquiry to enable educators, students and all citizens who see participatory learning as an effective means to the cultivation of a culture of peace, to work towards new concepts and policies of global, human security.

The framework of inquiry with which the group works has strong feminist roots, but also draws upon the constructive, analytic modes of masculine thinking that have produced some of the most promising proposed alternatives to war. They seek to develop partnerships in learning and action towards redefining security in human terms more consistent with the principles of non-violence, universal human dignity and sustainable living systems, the ethical core of the concept of a culture of peace. They have conceptualized human security as the expectation of human wellbeing and see the sources of wellbeing in the positive resolution of the four problems here identified as major obstacles to a culture of peace.

In sum, they see human security as the consequence of: (a) a healthy planet, providing a sustainable living environment; (b) the meeting of basic human needs for physical wellbeing and human development; (c) universal respect for and fulfilment of all human rights for all people; and (d) a renunciation of violence and armed conflict in favour of non-violent modes of struggle for change and conflict resolution. Their framework offers a comprehensive approach to the study of the problematic outlined in this section. The defining, mission statement of this group, the Women's International Network on Gender and Human Security, and some of the questions formulated for their inquiry provide a device for introducing issues of human security into peace education. Elements of both masculine and feminine thinking can be combined in an inquiry conducted in a partnership perspective that explores gender complementarity and possibilities for co-operation between women and men. It is hoped that all following this course of study will work towards further modes of learning and educating towards this same goal [30].

Foundational concepts

Problematique

This French term for a set of interrelated problems, viewed and addressed as a whole, is sometimes substituted with the English 'problematic' used as a noun. It is the basis for a mode of problem-solving consistent with the holism and process-based learning approaches advocated by peace education.

- ## Legitimate force

As defined above, legitimate force can be coercive and restraining, but seeks to avoid and minimize harm to all and in most cases cannot and does not become lethal. When force becomes violent by inflicting avoidable harm it is no longer legitimate. Force is legitimate when lawful or applied with the consent of the communities concerned.

- ## Transition

A process of going from one stage to another. Here it refers to part of the wider and deeper process of transformation, the changing of structures, systems and relationships that comprise societies and cultures. Transitional steps are intentional, incremental changes and strategies designed to lead towards the desired transformation.

- ## Feminist

Feminists adhere to the belief that women are equal to men and that it is necessary to change fundamental relationships and structures to achieve gender equality. Some now hold that deeper changes in cultures are also necessary.

- ## Ecofeminism

Ecofeminism is a convergence of feminism and environmentalism that argues that environmental destruction is the consequence of the technological thinking that characterizes Western patriarchy.

- ## Crimes against humanity

As defined above these crimes are violations of human rights that debase all of humanity. International legal norms categorize genocide, apartheid and torture as such crimes. Rape in war is now being addressed as a crime against humanity. Some argue that all sexual enslavement such as that imposed by the Japanese military in the Second World War, the 'rape camps' of Bosnia and enforced prostitution should be so categorized.

Learning processes and projects

Processes

Designing models; assessing alternatives; planning transition scenarios

1. Review the process of imaging a preferred future. Outside of class each student should spend some reflective time on the tasks listed in Item 2 below, and make notes to bring to a co-operative learning group.

2. Form co-operative learning groups to list the characteristics of an international security system that is non-violent and gender just, a system in which force is not used to inflict harm or damage, and men and women are socially, politically and economically equal. Think especially in terms of the kinds of public institutions, civil society organizations and gender relationships that would be necessary to realize the characteristics you outline. Conduct your discussion according to the following inquiry:

   • List and agree upon the characteristics and the values and principles which produce them. You can keep reporting notes in columns, listing them under the designations of 'characteristics,' 'values,' and 'principles'. (Think of principles as brief statements of the actualization of a value and allow a little more space in the column where you are noting them. Example: Violent force should not be used to achieve policy goals.)

   • What kind of conflict resolution procedures would be necessary to assure these characteristics? Describe the institutions that would carry them out, such as courts, mediation procedures, councils, itinerant teams for dispute resolution, etc. If such institutions are now in existence or proposed, indicate if and what changes in them you would propose.

- What kind of forces would be established to maintain order and assure that persons and nations do not harm each other? How would they be conscripted and trained?
- What kind of public institutions would you propose to realize and maintain assurance of each of the four sources of human security proposed in this section, that is, healthy environment; fulfilment of basic needs; respect for human rights; non-violent dispute resolution and positive, non-threatening relationships with others?
- What kind of civil society organizations would you propose to enable citizens to participate in public affairs and assure that governments are always kept aware of the needs and wishes of civil populations?

Note: These descriptions can be presented in verbal narratives or in the form of organizational charts such as those used to visually describe institutional components and relationships.

3. Report all groups' proposals to the entire class, starting with the characteristics lists. The entire class then discusses and agrees upon characteristics and principles they would all like to see in their preferred futures.
4. The class should use this agreed list of characteristics and principles as criteria to select from among the proposed public institutions and civil society organizations from which to construct common models of a global civil order that they believe might assure a preferred future in which a culture of peace would ultimately prevail in global society.
5. Once the class has agreed on a common model of institutions and organizations, they should resume group work to pursue an inquiry into a transition process of strategies to realize the

institutional images they have devised. The following questions
can be used to guide the inquiry and produce a 'transition
scenario' that can be used for actually planning a process of
change. This process is sometimes called 'backwards history' or
'futures projection'.

- What global conditions and international agreements
  regarding human security and gender justice would have to
  be in place in the few years prior to the actual inaugurations
  of the institutions and organization you have proposed,
  assuming it would be possible to achieve the transition
  within thirty years from the present?
- What conditions and agreements in the decade before that?
- What conditions would have to be achieved in the present
  decade? What actual positive developments and events
  should be fitted into your scenario? (i.e. the Optional
  Protocol to CEDAW, the International Criminal Court, etc.)
- Prepare a chronology of events that would have to take
  place to bring these conditions and agreements into being,
  starting with the next two years and ending with the official
  establishment of the proposed institutions.
- Outline the roles in this process of events that would be
  played by governments, civil society organizations,
  educational institutions and individual citizens.

6. Report the groups' scenarios to the entire class. Starting with the
   designation of actual present developments and events, devise a
   common scenario that the class agrees would be most likely
   possible. Discuss what citizens should do now to make it
   possible.

7. Resume group work to follow a similar process to outline a
   'framework of action for education for the achievement of
   human security in a gender just society of a culture of peace'.

8. Determine a scenario of action for educators and citizens to
   assure that schools and teacher-preparation institutions will
   undertake the actions outlined in your framework. Can this class
   take any such actions?

9. Students might enter in their journals some individual steps they

personally might take to work towards such education for a culture of peace in a gender perspective and for the realization of their preferred futures.

• Projects

1. Prepare teaching units for your expected students to introduce them to a holistic approach to and/or gender perspective on global problems as obstacles to a culture of peace.

2. Compare your class 'framework of action' with UNESCO's Integrated Framework and the UNESCO Associated Schools Project (http://www.unesco.org/education/asp). List ways in which your framework can strengthen and facilitate UNESCO's.

3. Consult The Hague Appeal for Peace Global Campaign for Peace Education website (http://www.haguepeace.org) to inquire into other possible efforts around the world to educate for a culture of peace in a gender perspective. Network with some of these educators to strengthen your mutual efforts and learn from each other.

Suggested readings

- **The Earth Charter**, http://www.eartcharter.org
- **World Survey on the Role of Women in Development**, *Globalizatio Gender and Work* (United Nations Publication, Sales # E.99.IV.8, Unite Nations, N.Y., 1999, ISBN 92-1-130200-5).
- **Background Paper** for UNESCO Consultation on Women's Contributio to a Culture of Peace, Manila, April, 1995. Available from Women and Culture of Peace Programme, UNESCO, Paris.
- **Vandana Shiva,** *Staying Alive, Women, Ecology and Development*, London, Zed Books, 1989 (ISBN 0-86232-823-3).
- **The Human Development Reports,** United Nations Development Programme, Human Development Report Office, New York (*Human Development Report*, published by Oxford University Press, Inc., New York, 1999).
- **Manfred B. Steger and Nancy S. Lind** (eds.), *Violence and Its Alternatives*, New York, St Martin's Press, 1999.
- **I. Breines, D. Gierycz and Betty A. Reardon** (eds.), *Towards a Wome Agenda for a Culture of Peace*, Paris, UNESCO, 1999.
- **V. Spike Peterson and Anne Sisson Runyon**, *Global Gender Issues*, 19 (ISBN 0-8133-6852-9).
- **Betty A. Reardon,** *Educating for Human Dignity: Learning About Hum Rights and Responsibilities*, Philadelphia, University of Pennsylvania Pre 1995.
- **All Human Beings, A Manual for Human Rights Education**, Paris, UNESCO Publishing, 1998.
- **Anne L. Barstow** (ed.), *War's Dirty Secret: Rape, Prostitution and Othe Crimes Against Women*, Cleveland, Ohio, Pilgrim Press, 2000.
  Note: A large selection of books on gender issues and gender analysis global problems is available from Women, Ink. 777 United Nations Plaz New York, NY 10017, e-mail: wink@womenink.org, website: http://www.womenink.org/
- A set of manuals for group work on the human rights of women, produced in all world regions is available from the People's Decade for Human Rights Education, 526 West 111th Street, New York, NY, 10025, USA. A list of documents related to UNESCO's Culture of Peace Programi can be accessed from the worldwide web at http://www.unesco.org/cp

PART TWO
Professional and pedagogical dimensions

Section 6
Attributes, capacities and skills of teachers of peace

• Educating to foster human capacities for peace-building

Part One of this study unit discussed suggestions for the foundations of education for a culture of peace. Those suggested foundations are: (a) primary characteristics of a culture of peace; (b) the formation of persons to function as responsible citizens in a social order characterized by peace, social justice and human equality; and (c) preparation to resolve the problems that present obstacles to realizing the vision of a culture of peace. Throughout those discussions, issues related to the ethical imperative of gender justice and the role of education in preparing citizens to solve global problems and create a culture of peace were considered.

Attributes, capacities and skills of teachers of peace

In Part Two, the discussion will be directed more specifically to relevant educational practices and institutions, and what will be required of teachers who take up the challenge of educating for a culture of peace in a gender perspective. As we previously addressed the social purposes of education for a culture of peace, and the capacities and skills that education must develop in citizens if those purposes are to be achieved, we will now deal with educational goals, teaching approaches, responsibilities of the schools and, first and most important, the professional qualities to be manifested and mastered by teachers of peace. The teacher is the most significant actor in authentic educational processes. The student is the central focus of the processes, and empowering the student as a responsible, creative learner is their objective.

Educational goals involving the fostering of human capacities for peace-building and constructive citizenship can be achieved best by teachers who have themselves developed capacities for the kinds of human and instructional interactions that the goals require. Skills training is imparted best by those who have themselves intentionally learned skills, understand their purposes and processes and the repeated efforts it takes to master them. Those preparing to educate for a culture of peace must be helped to develop the necessary capacities; and they must be guided through rigorous skills training. These capacities and skills will enable them to apply humanely and skilfully a range of teaching methodologies appropriate to the goals and consistent with the ethical principles of peace education. Teacher formation and the development of educating capacities; and teacher training and instruction for skills mastery – these are the two essential components of teacher education. This course of study seeks to guide those preparing teachers to educate for peace in peaceful learning communities in schools and other learning settings which in themselves can become spaces for a culture of peace.

• Some personal attributes of the teacher as a peace-builder and peace-maker

The teacher of peace needs to be a responsible global citizen, an intentional agent of a culture of peace, a person of vision, capable of hope and the imaging of positive change. Indeed, it is this latter attribute that inspires many to become teachers. For it is the attribute of hope, informed by preparation in the capacities and skills for facilitating change that lies at the heart of authentic education, its social purposes and the processes through which it seeks to elicit and develop human capacities for socially constructive and personally fulfilling lives. Teachers understand that education has always been a major agent of socially constructive change. The experience of teaching makes one realize that a socially constructive life is a personally fulfilling life.

Teaching is the most powerful and effective mode of learning. The professional preparation of teachers of peace will be most successful when the potential professionals come into the field out of motivations of service and love of learning: persons who see themselves as responsible to their societies, who are actively involved in their communities, and who relish the challenge of life-long learning. The teacher's self concept as a life-long learner is important in realizing the transformative power of education. It is a significant attribute of those who are able to view their own cultures from the reflective stance necessary to be both transmitter and transformer of cultures.

The role of teachers as transmitters of their traditional cultures is essential to maintaining the cultural continuity, integrity and diversity that would be a hallmark of a culture of peace. Teachers, more than any others, need to be steeped in a cultural tradition with a good knowledge at the history of their peoples and what events and forces have led them to change over time. For only on the basis of such knowledge viewed from the perspective of the values described as pertaining to a culture of peace can they be effective agents of transformation towards the full potential of their peoples to live in peace with those who are culturally different. Teachers can be the transformers of culture by being critical and reflective transmitters of culture in the spirit of lifelong learning.

The teacher of peace is a practitioner of peace and a seeker of the mutually enhancing relationships that nurture peace. The impulse to seek such relationships derives from profound respect for human worth and adherence to principles of human rights that should guide teacher/student relationships, and that is the foundation of a quality of interactions between them that are most conducive to learning. Self-respect and respect for others offer significant contributions to the effectiveness of teaching–learning processes. Observance of human-rights principles as the fundamental basis of classroom procedures and relationships leads to the democratic processes of participatory learning identified as integral to peace education. The teacher of peace is committed to human rights in principle and in practice.

Such a commitment is evident in the attributes of gender sensitivity and gender identification. The teacher of peace is sensitive to the process of gender identification which spans childhood and adolescence, and conducts her/himself so as to provide a model of both gender sensitivity and positive identification with the fundamental human worth, equal social value and special attributes of her/his own gender. The gender sensitive teacher relates to male and female students so as to help both form such positive identification for themselves and develop gender sensitivity towards others. Such a teacher inspires in students a shared vision of a gender-just, peaceful future.

The attribute of vision enables teachers to see the possibilities for positive development, not only in their societies, but also, and especially, in their students. From this perspective, a learning objective is an image of development in the learner and the learning plan a transition strategy intended to achieve it. Like other strategies for change, learning plans need to be assessed for effectiveness and amended when necessary. Firmness in values and goals and flexibility in methods and strategies are attributes of good teaching and ethical politics of change. Assessing and changing strategies and methods calls for constructive criticism. Teachers of peace are constructively critical of their societies and their students. They offer criticism so as not to wound or harm, but rather to elicit constructive change towards achieving proposed goals and objectives.

• Some professional capacities of a teacher of peace

These above-mentioned attributes form the basis of capacities that can be elicited and perfected through teacher education. Those following this course can engage in co-operative learning to help each other develop these capacities of learning and teaching and to understand that both processes are integral to the process we call education. With the facilitation provided by their instructor, they can help each other to develop some of the essential professional capacities for reflective learning, nurturing community, transformative inquiry, caring for learners as whole persons, and for gender sensitivity and responsibility.

If perceiving oneself to be a life-long learner is an essential attribute of the teacher of peace, then devotion to continually perfecting one's own learning abilities is an important capacity. Such a teacher reflects on teaching itself as a learning process, and education as a medium equally important for social and cultural transformation as it is for the transmission of social and cultural traditions. Teaching for transformation calls for learning daily how to understand the changing world, how to work with students to facilitate the development of their full learning capacities and how to act personally as well as professionally as an agent of change, remembering that learning is change in the learners.

Peaceful teachers have the capacity to establish and maintain relationships with students which provide them with confidence in the teachers' respect for their dignity and commitment to their learning. This capacity also extends to assuring mutual respect among students and to the ability to nurture a sense of community among students that enables them to become committed to the learning of all in the class. As noted earlier, co-operative learning is an effective route to the development of learning communities. Learning communities in themselves also enhance learning. Commitment to community is a powerful force for sustaining mutually enhancing relationships, for reinforcing respect for human dignity and creating a climate for the growth of a culture of peace. A culture of peace will grow community by community. And it is in the community that a culture of peace will be most likely first experienced. Teachers need to develop their capacities for creating a culture of peace as the classroom community of their students.

The teacher as learner is also the teacher as inquirer, one who has the capacity to pose instructive questions and to plan inquiries into the conditions that impede and those that enhance possibilities for achieving a culture of peace. The capacity to form a problematic is very useful when teaching is concerned with facilitating the transformative process of moving persons and societies along the path of a culture of peace. The articulation of problems to be solved in striving towards a goal, posing queries into potential solutions and then questions to assess the solutions is the mark of the teacher as inquirer. Caring and careful inquiry is a primary mode to peace learning. The teacher of peace is a caring inquirer.

Teachers of peace intentionally develop the capacity to care by knowing the learners in their charge as individuals, and by attending to them as such as well as students. This capacity is one that enables teachers to respond to the differences in students' personalities and learning styles as positively as they are expected to respond to other human differences. As cultural and other differences can be used to facilitate understanding of the multiple ways of being human, various interests and several learning styles are used by teachers of peace to orchestrate co-operative learning exercises that model the potential for problem-solving and peace-building that lie in multiple ways of thinking and learning.

A teacher of peace in attending to students as learners and caring for them as individuals, demonstrates capacities for both gender sensitivity and gender responsibility. In being sensitive to gender difference and alert to any possibility of gender bias in self or students, the teacher of peace is also gender-responsible. That responsibility is taken when teachers integrate gender differences in a positive manner that illuminates the complementarity that can exist between men and women and how each has distinct but significant contributions to make to the learning community as they do to the society. Gender responsibility is a capacity that leads teachers to deal critically and constructively with gender expectations, helping students to understand the humanizing as well as the limiting aspects of gender roles in their own and other cultures, leading them to reflect responsibly on what enriches and should be preserved for cultural continuity and what degrades and should be changed for cultural transformation. A gender-responsible teacher assures the equal participation of male and female students, and that all are heard respectfully and appreciated for their unique personal attributes.

A teacher of peace understands that a process leading to a global culture of peace is one of a life-affirming, humanizing balance between preservation and transformation, and that maintaining that balance in the classroom is a matter of professional skill. Responsible, effective teachers of peace are, therefore, ceaselessly broadening their skill repertoires, perfecting them through critical practice in community with other educators. Thus community building and co-operation are two significant characteristics of a culture of peace which teachers can derive from their professional capacities and develop through professional skill.

● **Professional skills of a teacher of peace**

As with the skills to be developed in learners, the skills of the teacher emerge from and realize their professional capacities. There is a wide range of skills to be employed in educating for a culture of peace in a

Attributes, capacities and skills of teachers of peace

gender perspective. The focus here will be on those necessary related to the capacities emphasized above, asserting that each set of skills; reflective learning, nurturing community, transformative inquiry, caring for the learner, gender sensitivity and responsibility are integral to a pedagogy of peace and gender justice.

The skills of reflective learning are those through which teachers apply what they learn from their teaching to the deepening of their understanding of their students and improving the learning processes they conduct so as to be as conducive as possible to achieving their teaching goals. These skills are essentially those of assessing one's own professional behaviours and abilities. Reflection on behaviours and abilities calls for self-questioning and assessment by posing some fundamental questions: What are the qualities of interactions I am conducting with my students? How effective are these teaching/learning interactions in achieving the learning goals that have been established? What indicators do I have that students are finding satisfaction and meaning in their learning? Am I interacting with all so as to honour their fundamental worth and help them to recognize their unique personal attributes? Do I observe gender equality and balance in conducting lessons and attending to students?

For experienced teachers this reflective learning on teaching practice is often an ongoing inner dialogue. Newer teachers and those who find it useful to have a record of their own professional growth might keep a journal on reflective professional assessment would be a very useful device, similar to that of students in this course keeping a conceptual journal to record the development of their conceptual understanding of issues and topics related to gender and a culture of peace. Journals might also be kept to record responses to and analysis of world developments related to gender and peace and personal reviews of readings that enable teachers to keep abreast of the field.

Nurturing community calls for some of the very skills of communication that teachers of peace seek to develop in their students as discussed in Section 4. It also calls for applying techniques to foster tolerance, mutual respect and co-operation in the classroom and to monitor intolerance and destructive competition in the learning environments for which a teacher is responsible, whether in a classroom, study hall, playing-field or off-campus school activities. A tool for monitoring intolerance, 'Some Symptoms of Intolerance and their Behavioral Indicators' can be found in *Tolerance – The Threshold of Peace* (hereafter referred to as *Tolerance*), Unit 1, p. 21. Applying this tool as with all other forms of monitoring requires skills of observation and interpretation. Teachers need to know what is actually transpiring among the class members and assess its meaning to relationships among students directly involved and its effects on the learning community of the class. Open communication between students and teachers is essential to this particular skill of peace-making and community. Skills of conflict resolution, as well as judgement about when and which types to apply, are other basic skills of community maintenance.

Community can be fostered in part through the practice of co-operative learning. In the formation of groups to perform the co-operative learning tasks, care should be taken to discourage any sense of negative competition or in-group-out-group behaviour among students. Teachers must be ever alert to picking up instances of moral exclusion in which students bring into the learning community discriminatory attitudes that rationalize exclusion of other class members. For this purpose, teachers may find helpful the behavioural indicators of bullying from *Tolerance*, Unit 2, p. 8, and the lesson plan, 'Bullyproof' on pp. 61–4 of Unit 1. To avoid moral exclusion or to transform such instances into constructive learning experiences, teachers will need to be skilled at fostering positive communication among students, at reflective listening and participatory hearing, and at clarifying the fundamental principles of human rights that form the basis of any just and democratic community. In this regard the lesson plans in *Tolerance*, Unit 2, pp. 65–8 on 'Learning to Live in Community' and 'Establishing Classroom Rights and Responsibilities' might be of help to teachers.

Attributes, capacities and skills of teachers of peace

Transformative inquiry skills are those that distinguish the
teachers of peace from those who teach primarily to instil
knowledge of the present rather than to inspire understanding of
possibilities for the future. A framework for conducting such an
inquiry was presented as the sample learning process in Section 2
with the imaging process, extended in Section 5 with model design
and transition planning. These process directions provide
procedures, but the success of the procedure in facilitating learning
about alternative possibilities for a culture of peace, and for
planning and acting to achieve such a culture, will depend upon
the skill with which the teacher leads the students through the
inquiry. The core of such an inquiry is three central questions:
What kind of a world do we want? What changes need to be made
to achieve it? What are our social responsibilities to initiate and
carry out the transformation process? All others are essentially
subsidiary questions to these core questions.

The task of the teacher is to help students and facilitate their
helping each other to comprehend that futures are made; they don't
simply happen. They are the consequence of human imagination
and human will. If we can imagine a positive alternative, have a
commitment to its realization, and can work co-operatively with
others to plan and carry out a process of transition, we can
transform the world. Transformation, then, is a matter of
imagination, commitment, co-operation and skill; the main skill
being asking the relevant and productive questions about the
process of achieving a preferred future of peace and gender justice.
What do we need to know? How do we act on our knowledge?
Where can we find the information and how can we acquire the
skills? How can we work with others pooling our knowledge and
skills to fulfil our common commitment, that is, how can we build
transformative learning communities?

To conduct this inquiry around specific goals and particular
issues, teachers need above all the skills of elicitation, to draw from
the students their own visions and ideas. They need to be able to
respond to students' statements with encouraging and ever probing
questions or eliciting questions which facilitate students' delving

deeper into their own knowledge and imaginations to fill out the details of the kind of future they prefer and how they propose to achieve it. Students should be guided to reason more fully in proposing alternatives and transition strategies. Teachers should be more raisers of interesting, reflective and productive questions than givers of answers. They should become skilful at the art of formulating and posing what might be called 'queries' rather than questions. Questions can be answered with statements of fact. Queries demand reflective, reasoned responses. Answers close questions. Responses carry the inquiry forward into further learning, revealing further possibilities for empowerment and change.

The way in which inquiry and discussions are conducted and lessons presented in the classroom is one of the means through which teachers manifest the care for the learner as a whole person.

Clearly most teachers already carry a heavy burden of responsibility in presenting the curriculum. Extra functions may seem only to add to that burden. However, the values that underlie education for a culture of peace and the success of efforts to impart it depend in large part on a mutually enhancing relationship between teachers and students. Skills of caring, and taking the time to apply them, are integral to the learning process of education for peace. Attention to students' emotional state and physical wellbeing can help assure their readiness to learn. Caring and supportive behaviour from teachers lets students know they are valued as individuals and can contribute to their sense of self-worth as they learn the caring skills and behaviours modelled by teachers. Some teachers even start the school day or the class with a wellbeing or 'How are we all doing?' check, asking students to report any news they want to share or acknowledge something they would like others to be sensitive to that day.

Such checks can also be conducted periodically during a learning sequence to determine students' own assessment of their learning. Giving an opportunity to express difficulties or needs for clarification from the teacher and classmates can facilitate the learning process and demonstrate that the teacher truly cares about the students and their learning.

Attention to students' learning styles and special talents and difficulties can help teachers to form co-operative learning groups in which students can practise care for the learning of others when the group is organized with a complementary balance of learning gifts and learning needs. Such attention also helps teachers to formulate queries and responses most likely to facilitate the learning of particular students. As one learns the interests and gifts of friends to enrich friendships and enliven conversations, teachers can learn of these qualities in their students to enrich the learning process and enliven classes. Cultures of peace are likely to be derived from lively conversations in learning communities. Communities are built through care for and commitment to the wellbeing of those with whom we seek to build community.

Building gender-just learning communities also calls for special professional skills. Teachers can intentionally develop skills to assure gender-sensitive and gender-responsible behaviour in their preparation, to be further refined and varied through classroom practice. Throughout this unit we have referred to the qualities that make for gender sensitivity and have noted some of the behaviours that manifest gender responsibility. These qualities and behaviours are the basis of a skills repertoire teachers can apply to the establishment and maintenance of a gender-just classroom. Clearly describing and acknowledging in a positive way some of the differences between boys' and girls' learning styles and problem-solving, pointing out how these enrich the communal learning process and extend the range of problem-solving methods available to the whole class, is a skilful manifestation of gender sensitivity.

Leading students through a consideration of how these differences have often led to educational discrimination, most often against girls, but also in various instances against boys, demonstrates how gender discrimination instils the limiting notion that there is only one correct way to accomplish a task. This is an important learning task for the practice of gender responsibility. Structuring lesson plans and co-operative learning tasks so that male and female students can attempt any learning task that interests them regardless of gender is another skill of gender responsibility that manifests the principle that equality is not sameness. It is renouncing negative discrimination. It is a skill of task construction that can bring gender responsibility into any social, economic or political process. Gender-just task construction certainly should be standard practice in peace-making, peace-building and imaging and creating cultures of peace.

• Foundational concepts

The definitions below are given in pairs because each concept must be considered with reference to the other in the pair in order to comprehend in it in the context within which it is used in this unit.

• Formation and training

These are two fundamental and integral aspects of teacher education. Formation is the aspect which builds on personal attributes and qualities to elicit professional capacities for development. Training is the process of skill development which involves instruction through descriptions, explanations and modelling by teacher educators and practice with other student teachers.

• Education and indoctrination

Education is the systematically planned, guided learning that develops the potential talents and capacities of learners and opens them to reflective thinking, responsible action and life-long learning. Indoctrination is direct, specific instruction in one mode of thinking, communicating to learners that there is only one good way to learn, to be human and to achieve social purposes.

Attributes, capacities and skills of teachers of peace

Education is pursued by democracy, and indoctrination by authoritarianism. The former may lead to tolerance and respect for human rights, the latter to intolerance and moral exclusion.

• Commitment and community

Commitment is dedication to act to realize one's own and one's society's principles, values and goals. Such action is often taken communally, in concert with others. Communities, groups that share common values and seek common goals, are sustained through the commitment of their members. This is true of learning communities as well as other forms of community.

• Participatory learning and empowerment

Learning by doing is a means by which learners become aware of their own capacities and skills and come to appreciate that they have abilities through which to achieve their own goals and contribute to those of their communities. Learning for empowerment of the citizenry is a goal of education for democracy.

• Learning gifts and learning needs

Every person has unique characteristics that influence the ways in which he or she learns. Some of these characteristics facilitate certain learning tasks while presenting difficulties in others. Teachers of peace and gender justice, through co-operative learning groups and other such caring methods of teaching, try to assure that learning gifts are used to the advantage of the particular learners and to enrich the learning of others, while attempting to meet individual learning needs and guiding students in helping to meet each other's needs.

• Questions and queries

The inquiries which comprise peace education are based on queries, questions which pose learning tasks and raise other questions in pursuit of the task to deepen and extend learning. Questions are devices for eliciting facts and information needed to pursue the inquiry opened by a query.

• Learning processes and projects

• Process

Role-play

Role-plays are effective devices for demonstrating some of the attributes, capacities, and skills of teaching and caring. Among them are empathy and perspective taking, appreciation of how another feels and an understanding of how they view the world and particular situations.

Create a series of role plays based on actual classroom situations involving teacher/student relations and communications and student/student relations and communication that will help to illuminate various possibilities for practising and perfecting the attributes, capacities and skills outlined above. Think of various alternative responses to the situation presented.

After each role-play, invite others in the class to play the roles in different ways. Discuss which ways were most conducive to creating a peaceful classroom and why they were so. Analyse the perspectives and positions of each of the actors in the role-plays. Note especially aspects related to gender and power.

Role-plays can also be used in conflict resolution and problem-solving as they are in Augusto Boal's *Theatre of the Oppressed* and in LEAP, a London-based programme that uses improvisational theatre to teach about conflict resolution (Leaveners' Conflict Resolution Training, 8 Lennox Road, Finsbury Park, London N4 3NW, United Kingdom).

Suggested readings

- **Mary Belenky et al.,** *Women's Ways of Knowing: The Development of Self, Voice, and Mind*, New York, Basic Books, 1997.
- **Edgar Faure** (ed.), *Learning to Be: The World of Education Today and Tomorrow*, Paris, UNESCO Publishing, 1982.
- **Betty A. Reardon,** *Educating the Educators: The Preparation of Teachers for a Culture of Peace* (Peace Education Miniprints, No. 99, School of Education, Sweden, May 1999).
- **Our Creative Diversity**, Report of the World Commission on Culture and Development, Paris, UNESCO Publishing, 1997.

Recommended research

Conduct interviews with those responsible for curricular planning for the teacher-education institution in which you are enrolled and other institutions you may have access to. Gather information on the social and professional priorities that inform the choice of curricular topics and criteria of professional competence.

Assess the suitability of these topics and criteria to education for a culture of peace in a gender perspective. If you conclude that changes should be made, draft recommendations, describing the changes fully and providing a rationale for the statement and suggestions for preparations and implementation of each recommendation.

Section 7:

Learning goals of education for a culture of peace

Preparatory readings

Tolerance – The Threshold of Peace, Unit 1, Chapter 4, pp. 52–4, for Teacher Training, 'General Learning Goals: Values, Knowledge and Skills', Unit 2 for Primary Schools, Chapter 4, 'Learning Goals of Education for Peace, Human Rights and Democracy', pp. 21–4, and Unit 3 for Secondary schools, Chapter 4, 'Learning Goals of Education for Peace, Human Rights and Democracy', pp. 27–30.

This syllabus has made extensive use of *Tolerance* to illustrate some alternative forms of approaches to educating for goals normatively and substantively related to the purposes to be served by this study unit. *Tolerance* contains many practical lesson plans which can be adapted to the goals and objectives proposed here, serving as models for planning lessons for education for a culture of peace in a gender perspective. It also contains suggestions for discussion. By shifting the focus of those questions, especially those offered in the sections assigned as preparatory reading for this section, from tolerance to peace and gender justice you will have an appropriate guide to discussion of this and other sections of this study unit. In the charts and texts of the three *Tolerance* units you will find enrichment of the material offered here. You will also find two other significant elements for the systematic planning of peace education, proposals for a developmentally based curricular sequence from kindergarten to secondary school and samples of a process and participatory pedagogy advocated as a means to achieve the reforms and developments in educational practice called for by the Integrated Framework of Action on Education for Peace, Human Rights and Democracy.

The learning goals of education for a culture of peace, an extension of learning goals for tolerance identified as a 'threshold' or first-stage learning goal of peace education, are both social and personal. Deriving from a set of social values that would be manifest in a culture of peace, these goals are described here in terms of capacities attributed to persons formed by and conscious of the need to strive to achieve and be ever vigilant of the need for responsibility to maintain a culture of peace.

Among the core values giving rise to the social norms and legal standards of a social order in a culture of peace are environmental sustainability, cultural integrity/diversity, human solidarity, social responsibility and gender equality. These values designate what the society that embraces them deems to be conditions that are intrinsically good and worth striving for; any measure achieved to be vigilantly maintained. The striving and maintaining will be the result of the application of skills deriving from the cultivation of the fundamental human capacities that inspire the values, skills informed by knowledge gained, certainly through experience, the most important being learning experience guided by a pedagogy of peace.

Each of these capacities can serve as a basis for comprehension of cognitive knowledge and can be developed into a range of skills through the various pedagogies that have been devised or adapted by peace education. Some of these are suggested in the matrix of Goals and Methods on pp. 158-61. Here the values and capacities, the related skills and relevant knowledge and a selected list of pedagogic methods are presented in relationship one to the other. A form demonstrates a holistic overview of the conceptual goals of the values and capacities as they relate to some of the skills and knowledge learning objectives and some of the teaching methods suited to the goals and objectives. Please study and discuss this matrix, comparing it with the various related charts in *Tolerance*.

● Foundational concepts

Values	Capacities
Environmental sustainability. Preserving the life sustaining capacity of the earth.	*Ecological awareness*. Noting and responding to needed action to maintain the health of Planet Earth.
Cultural integrity/diversity. Respect for the unique human qualities of all cultures. Respect for the diversity of human cultures.	*Cultural proficiency*. Appreciation of cultural differences and ability to function socially in another (other) cultures(s).
Human solidarity. Awareness that all humans are one species and a commitment to the wellbeing of humanity.	*Global agency/engagement*. Acting as a global citizen to resolve global problems, and achieve a culture of peace.
Social responsibility. Taking action for the wellbeing of the community and improvement of society.	*Conflict competence*. The capacity and skills to resolve conflicts justly and to engage in reconciliation.
Gender equality. Assurance of the equal human worth and dignity of women and men.	*Gender sensitivity*. Appreciation of differences between, and unique qualities of, women and men and the ability to note and take action when differences are the basis of discrimination of any kind.

● Matrix of goals and methods

See pp. 158-61. Instructors and students are encouraged to construct and extend their own matrices.

● Learning processes and projects

● Process

Values assessments

Many of the most significant personal values we hold are neither thoroughly assessed, nor put to a test of ethical standards or effectiveness as guides to behaviour. Some of the most important social values also go untested, being taken for granted or considered to be too time-honoured and culturally unchallengeable to discuss openly. A number of these values relate to war and gender. This unit has attempted to encourage those who study it to become more self-conscious of personal values and socially conscious of social and cultural values so that education can assure that the most positive values are enhanced and the negative ones are transformed. The following inquiry offers one approach to an exploration and assessment of values.

Values inquiry

Form co-operative learning groups and assign each group one of the five fundamental values listed in the Matrix of Goals and Methods on pp. 158-61. The group is to prepare a value assessment according to the following inquiry:

- How is this value honoured, ignored or violated in our society and local community?
- What concrete examples can serve as indicators of the value in operation?
- How does the school and the curriculum manifest the value?
- Are there any ways in which the school or the curriculum contributes to the violation or ignoring of the value?
- What can we conclude about how important our society, community and schools consider this value to be?

Report the conclusions to the class and follow with a discussion of how the class as educators should respond to these conclusions. Some may want to write journal entries to do personal assessments of the five values.

• Projects

Select two or more of the skills and categories of knowledge listed in the Matrix of Goals and Methods. On the basis of the general objectives listed in the matrix, draw up some specific learning objectives suitable to the students you will be teaching and then design some lesson plans to achieve them. Form co-operative learning groups to test your lesson plans with your peers.

Design a developmental curricular sequence for teaching about gender tolerance and gender equality for all elementary and secondary grades. Arrange your plan in a matrix containing: grade level; tolerance and gender-equality concepts to be taught; significant values to be communicated; problems to be studied; and teaching approaches to be used.

Discuss the following queries and questions as you prepare the design. If children and adolescents are to learn to be tolerant and gender-just persons, what are some of the values they must hold? What concepts will enable them to understand problems of intolerance and gender discrimination and to live by the values of justice you have identified? What problems must they be aware of? How might they have experienced some of these problems at various ages? What teaching approaches would be most effective at each grade level to teach these concepts, values and problems? Arrange your plans in the matrix and use it to guide the development of future lesson plans.

Suggested readings

- **Birgit Brock Utne**, *Educating for Peace, a Feminist Perspective*, New York, Teachers College Press, 1994 (The Athene Series).
- **Betty A. Reardon**, *Comprehensive Peace Education: Educating for Global Responsibility*, New York, Teachers College Press, 1988.
- **Alicia Cabezudo**, et al., *Learning to Abolish War: A Teaching Manual*, New York, The Hague Appeal for Peace, 2001.

Recommended research

Review the learning goals for citizenship education set forth by the education authority under which you will teach. Are these goals compatible with and/or adequate to education for a culture of peace in a gender perspective? How will you deal with discrepancies?

Matrix of goals and methods

Values	Capacities	Skills	Knowledge	Pedagogy
Environmental sustainability Concern for the health of the planet and human responsibility for maintaining it	**Ecological awareness** Knowledge inspired by concern and understanding of the earth as a single system and humanity's part of the system, responsible for its health	Analyse components and functions of biosystems Assess consequences of human behaviours and social policy to the environment Gender analysis and economic and social analysis of environmental policies	Knowledge of major crises of air, water, topsoil, natural resources Knowledge of nature and limits of sustainable development Knowledge of impact of military and industrial activity on the environment Knowledge of gender roles in relation to environment	Observation of living ecosystems Study of the biosphere Study of environmental policies Research into the positions of environmental advocacy groups Ethical reflection on environmental policies and behaviours
Cultural integrity/ diversity Respect for cultural difference and role of culture in human identity and fulfilment	Cultural proficiency Knowledge of and ability to function positively in one or several other cultures	Cultural interpretation Social skills in another culture Converse in another language Taking the perspective of another culture	Knowledge of the history, values, worldviews and beliefs of another culture Knowledge and understanding of myths of origin and meaning of another culture	Readings about and discussion of other cultures Cultural interpretations of the arts and literature of other peoples Gender interpretation of literature and films of another people

Values	Capacities	Skills	Knowledge	Pedagogy
			Knowledge and understanding of gender roles and gender formation	Interactions with representatives of another culture
				Observation of others' holidays and feast days
			Attitudes toward war, violence, and force	Museum visits
Human solidarity Observing the unity of all humanity as a single species and as a unit of moral inclusion, including a commitment to justice and ethical treatment of others	**Global agency/ engagement** Comprehension of various problems of violence in world society as interrelated elements of the culture of war	Critical analysis and gender interpretation of global problems	Nature and extent of global problems	Documentary films and readings on the problems
			International Human Rights Standards	Study advocacy materials published by NGOs
		Local organizing techniques for action on global problems		
			United Nations Declaration and policy statements on global problems	Discussion and position taking on issues
	Ability to think critically about the culture and the problems and participate in global civil society	Means to apply international standards to local and national problems		Pursuing critical arguments
			Movements and organizations active in global civil society	Simulations of policies and alternative solutions
		International networking		
				Volunteering and interning for organizations and agencies
		Lobbying at all levels		

Learning goals of education for a culture of peace

Values	Capacities	Skills	Knowledge	Pedagogy
Social responsibility Commitment to universal human rights and responsibility for defending and implementing them with a sense of personal accountability to society	**Conflict competency** Ability to conduct conflict and struggle for positive change constructively Engage in democratic controversial discourse, resist injustice, resolve conflict, reconcile and reconstruct relationships	Identify and formulate alternatives Articulate positions on issues and alternatives, and criticisms of policies antithetical to peace values Argue in favour of a position or alternative Conflict resolution Reconciliation Reconstruction	Fluent command of one's own language Dynamics of formation, processes of conflict escalation and dissipation or resolution Laws governing conflicts and citizen responsibilities Theory and practice of non-violence	Simulations of conflicts Practice of resolution skills and processes Identifying steps of reconciliation Visits to courts and mediation agencies Providing resolution services for other students Service learning
Gender equality Commitment to the equal value of women and men rooted in the value of universal human dignity. Belief that gender balance should prevail in all social institutions and human relationships based on concept of	**Gender sensitivity** Behaviors that provide equal opportunities and honour both the similarities and differences between men and women Avoidance of gender stereotyping and limiting human	See issues and problems from perspectives of both men and women, boys and girls Recognize stereotypes; observe their inaccuracies and limitations Use of gender-inclusive	Knowledge of origins and formation of gender roles Cultural variations in gender roles and perceptions of masculine and feminine Negative consequences of devaluing or	Keeping journals on personal gender experiences Readings in gender studies and women's issues Study of women's movements and international standards

161

Values	Capacities	Skills	Knowledge	Pedagogy
complementarity	achievement on basis of sex as a form of injustice Seeking partnerships between men and women based on complementarity and mutual enhancement	language for general references to human beings Analyse differences, similarities and complementarities in a cultural context	repressing one gender or privileging one – specific knowledge of oppression of women Positive consequences of equality, mutuality, and complementarity	on women's rights Role-plays of 'gender incidents' from both perspectives

Section 8

Teaching approaches to educating for a culture of peace from a gender perspective

Preparatory readings

• **Betty A. Reardon, Tolerance – the Threshold of Peace**, Unit 3 for Secondary Schools, Chapter 2, 'Responding to a Major Problem of Adolescent Intolerance: Bullying', pp. 1–22, Chapter 3, 'Suggested Content for a Process Approach to Learning the Realms of Tolerance at the Secondary-school Level', pp. 23–6.

• The process and participatory orientation of peace education

As can be seen from the pedagogies listed in the Matrix of Goals and Methods, there are multiple ways in which teaching for a culture of peace in a gender perspective can be approached. Throughout this unit, the suggested learning processes and projects have demonstrated some of the methods peace educators have devised as the basis of participatory and process learning. Each of these learning processes can be adapted to all levels of elementary and secondary education. Each can be integrated into a comprehensive and developmental approach to education for peace in a gender perspective.

In this section, the focus will be on several of those learning processes that hold most promise with regard to the social purposes of decreasing violence in all its forms and increasing social justice and gender equality.

• Discussion

At the centre of these methods is reflective, reasoned discussion, the first method outlined in Section 1. Discussion must be built on knowledge and information. Sound substantive content is the foundation of peace education. Participation in process learning is one of the most effective ways for learners to integrate and gain adequate command of content. Informed discourse is both an effective learning device and the means by which communities arrange their lives and plan their futures. Capacity to engage in well-reasoned, factually based discussion is a core goal of peace education which leads to the use of participatory discussion as a teaching method.

• Imaging

Imaging a preferred future, the method described in Section 2, is more than an exercise imagining desirable futures. It is a device to enable learners to discern and describe possibilities. Possibilities are the raw material from which a preferred future can be fashioned, peace can be made and hope can be inspired. Without hope, citizens have little motivation to work for a culture of peace. Projecting a future of peace, designing models of institutions to maintain peace and assure justice, planning transition strategies to bring them into being are exercises that give learners experience in problem-solving, issues analysis and some of the most essential skills of responsible citizenship. Teaching methods that cultivate the imagination, disciplined by the skills outlined here, are well suited to education for change. Preparation for change and responsible citizenship in global civil society is a major social purpose of peace education.

• Perspectives

Perspective-taking helps students to understand the values and world views of others by looking at situations and issues from various perspectives. As indicated in Section 3, it is also a device for developing empathy, a capacity at the root of caring, as well as a means through which multiple and alternative possibilities can be discerned. Perspective-taking is both a teaching method and a skill to be applied to problem-solving and conflict resolution. Observing and assessing a condition, situation or an event from the positions and perspectives of other political beliefs, economic circumstances, cultures or genders brings deeper understanding of the problems and clarifies what is at stake in a conflict. It is a skill to be perfected when seeking to develop the capacities of gender sensitivity and cultural proficiency and to realize the value of gender equality in our classrooms and our societies.

• Listening

Reflective listening and participatory hearing. The method presented in Section 4 provides an avenue for the development of caring skills and assures that discussions are clear, open and constructive. When the emphasis is on understanding before responding and on clarifying before challenging, all exchanges are more productive and relationships more mutually enhancing. Listening and hearing skills can help students to build positive, empathetic and mutually enhancing relationships in all spheres of personal and social life and in the fulfilment of economic and political responsibilities.

• Alternatives

Assessing alternatives and planning transition scenarios, as indicted in Section 5, are important learning devices for understanding and solving problems, especially problems such as those outlined in that section. They develop imaginative capacities and encourage learners to think in terms of multiple possibilities, transcending the dualistic mode of problem-posing and viewing policies and conflicts that characterizes the culture of war and violence. Thinking in the dualistic terms of either one particular way or another limits both the human imagination and social possibilities for problem-solving. Education has tended to cultivate adversarial discourse, the win–lose mode of debate, closing off possibilities for discussion towards common conclusions.

• Role-play

Role plays, as outlined in Section 6, like perspective taking, enable us to see from other vantage points, to understand how and why others might respond differently than we do to problematic situations. It makes possible consideration of alternative behaviours and how the alternatives might affect outcomes. It gives the learners involved an opportunity 'to get the feel' of a situation, to acquire effective understanding that enriches cognitive knowledge. It also enables learners to comprehend the emotional dimensions of crucial or controversial issues that are so often omitted in the dominant mode of problem-solving. It is a way of also introducing 'feminine' elements towards gender balance and a more fully human approach to problem-solving and conflict resolution. Devices such as switching roles, changing outcomes and other variations demonstrate the significance of choice and multiple possibilities in any human situation.

• Values assessment

Values assessment, the process suggested in Section 7, has been in some instances a very controversial approach. Communities, religious institutions and parents are sometimes fearful that the schools will usurp their roles in guiding the moral development of the young. In most cases, this is a fear based on the assumption that education is primarily instructive, inculcating rather than eliciting learning, and that values and moral education are conveyed more by precept than by open inquiry and informed reflection. Gender injustice and violence are the consequence of a failure to recognize ways in which societies continue to tolerate the violation of the fundamental values the world community acceded

to in the adoption of the Universal Declaration of Human Rights.
This failure is one element of the reluctance of many to examine
the values and assumptions that underlie public policies and
personal behaviour.

Reflection on one's own values and the behaviours they
inspire is basic to becoming the kind of person education for a
culture of peace seeks to form. Assessing the values of one's society
and the public policies that arise from them is essential to
responsible citizenship and a primary part of the process of
transition to a culture of peace. The projection of positive change
in both personal and social realms is impossible without clarity
about the values that provoke the change and the values that
inform the goals sought in the realization of a culture of peace. All
peace education is values based, and this syllabus, built around the
core values outlined in Section 7, has woven throughout it values
related to the ethical core of the international norms established by
the United Nations.

• Pursuing an inquiry

The suggested learning process in Section 8, constructing
frameworks of inquiry, is a mechanism for establishing goals,
clarifying concepts and pursuing the knowledge necessary to
achieving the goals. This syllabus has been constructed as a kind of
conceptual map of the necessities of and possibilities for education
for a culture of peace in a gender perspective. It has suggested
focusing on and discussing the concepts that are the very
foundation of the course of study outlined here. Discussion of the
concepts helps to raise questions and queries about meaning and
application in order that the concepts be properly understood and
appropriately applied. Discussion and inquiry are complementary
and integral to the participatory teaching approach favoured by
peace education.

Questions and queries are the most effective instigators of
learning. When arranged and posed in a coherent conceptual
framework of inquiry, they become the tools through which

problems can be defined and solutions can be pursued. Course designs, especially those dealing with social problems and/or controversial issues, based on such frameworks can be very effective in nurturing autonomous learners. The learning process at the end of this section is an example of such a framework.

• Contending issues

Constructive/creative contention is a form of discourse for addressing controversies and conflicts in a way consistent with and conducive to honouring the value of universal human dignity and realizing a culture of peace. It recognizes that a form of violence can be committed in words and forms of address that are intended to wound, forms often used in the adversarial way in which public issues are assessed and resolutions to conflicts sought. Adversarial discourse is encouraged in education when debate is taught as the primary way of resolving policy differences, and denigration and refutation is often the manner of dealing with an opposing argument. Debates conducted with respect and civility can be helpful in clarifying issues, but they seldom lead to resolutions fully satisfying to all involved. Education for peace seeks to move the discourse of argument and controversy out of the 'win or lose' realm into that of mutually conducted searches for the best solutions for all involved in any problematic situation, or at least one to which all would give their consent. As a teaching approach, constructive/creative contention seeks to contextualize differences as alternatives to be explored as well as disputes to be resolved. It is a positive means of honing argumentation skills in the pursuit of a common truth rather than competing to be 'right'.

To the foregoing eight approaches, three more will be suggested here, with the suggestions that those others in the Matrix of Goals and Methods also be reviewed for possibilities for trials with colleagues and classmates. Those three are: (a) problem-solving; (b) conflict processing; and (c) social action. Each of these holds positive potential as a teaching approach to education for a culture of peace in a gender perspective.

• Problem-solving

The most important element in problem-solving, especially when the problems relate to gender and/or violence, is that all involved in the problem come to see it as a mutual or common concern that has negative, if different, effects on all. Problems should be addressed as situations that are harmful to a community or a relationship. In so far as peace education encourages a holistic perspective, all aspects of the problem, as well as all who are directly and indirectly affected, should participate in proposing alternatives and selecting a solution.

As a general rule, teachers when using a problem-solving approach should encourage students to devise and propose multiple possibilities, as they consider the various aspects of the problem. Proposed solutions should be subject to values assessment and to questions about how all involved may be affected by the various proposed solutions. Proposal feasibility should also be explored, raising questions about whether the resources and knowledge necessary to their implementation are available.

Some of these questions are likely to be the basis of queries calling for further inquiry before a selection is made. Teachers should help students to understand that effective and ethical problem-solving usually requires extensive inquiry and reflection. The framework suggested below as a learning process demonstrates how problem queries give rise to other questions and queries in the search for the knowledge and understanding necessary to resolve the problem. Problem-solving should be viewed as a dynamic process rather than a static formula or recipe.

The problem most relevant to the concerns of this syllabus is violence, and the aspect of violence most crucial to the gender/ violence relationship is violence against women. This is a problem that negatively affects both boys and girls. Boys are more involved in various violent activities than girls. Teenage boys in North America, for instance, constitute a very high percentage of the victims as well as the perpetrators of violence. Violence against women is part of a complex of violence committed primarily by boys and men. Some researchers believe it to be the consequence of male socialization that must be addressed by education. Some educators are now doing so. In addition, the socialization of boys has recently been researched and analysed as one of the significant contributing factors in male violence against women.

This problem has been the subject of a number of teaching tools devised to deal with forms of gender bias that leave women and girls vulnerable to harassment and physical violence. There are curricula directed to both boys and girls to alert them to this problem and how to respond to it. A number of these curricula deal with the empowerment of girls through exercises to develop self worth and a capacity to avoid or deflect violence. There are also a few excellent curricula addressed to issues related to the socialization of boys. Two are listed below as suggested readings.

One of them, emphasizing the fundamental peace principle of positive human relationships, is entitled *Healthy Relationships: A Violence Prevention Curriculum* [25]. It was developed by Men for Change in Canada, and deals with a range of issues that produce sexist violence in North American culture. It is also applicable to a European context, and has some relevance to other cultures. Among the negative influences that contribute to sexist socialization, it cites the media as especially culpable. Media awareness is being developed to help students perceive and evaluate the images and messages of violence and gender violence they regularly encounter on radio, television, and at the cinema, as well as in comics and other print media.

Another important aspect of problem-solving related to violence and gender bias is anger management, or social and emotional learning. *Healthy Relationships* contains some useful teaching material for this purpose. Examples of their curricula may be found on the website listed in the references [25]. Educators for Social Responsibility, an American peace education organization, has also produced a number of curricular materials for social and emotional learning intended to provide education for greater life satisfaction through the development of emotional health and social responsibility (ESR, 475 Riverside Drive, New York, NY 10115, United States of America).

The project 'It is Fun to be Nice', Krokelvdal School, Tromso, Norway, one of the 6,000 UNESCO Associated Schools, has had excellent results from its positive reinforcement project. Further information on this project can be obtained on the Internet at: http://www.unesco.org/cpp/wcp/.

The gender and/or violence problematic can also be approached through the problem of the exclusion of women's peace-making capacities from most of the official peace nego-tiations. Adult non-formal educators are now addressing this issue, as are many women's peace organizations. Some of the training materials they are developing to prepare women to assert their rights and talents in peace-making are readily adaptable to classroom situations. One such material produced by UNESCO and the Forum of African Women Educators, *Promoting Women's Participation in Conflict Resolution to Build a Culture of Peace*, provides instruction in conflict resolution procedures primarily geared towards post-conflict reconciliation and healing processes [26].

• Conflict processing

Conflict and conflict resolution, as noted previously, are part of a more complex process. We have asserted that skills for constructive, non-violent participation in that process are basic life skills for living in a culture of peace and are essential to the transition process that will bring that culture into being. Because we see these as process skills, we refer to this approach as conflict processing, rather than conflict resolution. Many practitioners, however, still use the latter term to mean much of the general process we suggest here as a framework for education for and about conflict. This framework considers, before and after the resolution, a number of other phases in the conflict process that include anticipation of a conflict as a prior phase and post-conflict resolution reconciliation, restoring or establishing between the conflicting parties positive, mutually enhancing relationships, the essence of peace. The experience of post-conflict situations of the last two decades of the twentieth century have taught us that reconciliation represents a challenge to skills development of the same dimensions as that which produced the range of skills and methods now available for conflict resolution. Learning units to teach some of these skills of resolution and reconciliation appear in all three units of *Tolerance – The Threshold of Peace*, demonstrating that education for conflict processing can be introduced at all levels of education.

Conflict Processing Framework [27] describes the stages of a conflict-processing framework as devised by the Teachers College Curriculum Team of the Global Campaign for Peace Education. This and other relevant curricular materials appear on the Campaign's website with a call for further inquiry into the conflict analysis and pedagogical planning that will be required to develop curricula to assure effective teaching of all conflict-processing skills. The desired result of the process is conflict transformation, a concept previously defined. The term and the nature of the phases described suggest the normative nature of the process, which makes it a good basis for some forms of moral education. Many peace educators advocate moral education as a component of peace education, asserting that it should have a place in curricula related to human rights as well as peace and gender. The development of peace education itself is still in process. Ethical problem-solving and conflict-processing, including the goal of transformation and the skills of reconciliation, are two of the areas of endeavour to which the present generation of peace educators are called upon to contribute with innovative practices.

• Social action and service learning

Social action as a form of participatory learning is now practised in civic education as well as in peace education. Applied learning and learning by doing are two very effective approaches to an education that seeks to develop social responsibility and the capacity of global engagement and agency. Students who participate in social-service programmes are given a hands-on experience in responsibility and caring, and an opportunity to learn the value of service as a means of contributing to the wellbeing of the community. Such a value, as previously stated, should inform all education, including political, economic and social education. Through service learning, young people can learn the ways in which their work can contribute to the wellbeing of others and experience the satisfaction of making a positive difference to their communities. When such service is to individuals or groups who have suffered some form of violence, such as spousal or child abuse, homelessness or hunger, students learn experientially about these problems and have occasion to reflect on them and consider possibilities for social change.

Active, experiential learning in the realm of social change can reinforce positive social values and provide an experience of social or political efficacy that empowers learners to take more constructive action for change. Examples of such actions are students campaigning for the land-mines treaty, various environmental actions, working through human-rights advocacy groups such as Amnesty International for the relief of the suffering of victims of human-rights abuses, and various other social actions and services. Human-rights organizations and social-service agencies, especially those working on gender and/or violence issues, offer opportunities to arrange for service learning. When teams of students assigned to a variety of such organizations and agencies later share their learnings with classmates, a rich and varied learning experience is made available to the entire class.

One very appropriate and powerful possibility is offered by the White Ribbon Campaign, a Canadian initiated movement of 'men against violence against women'. The *Education and Action Kit* they devised for schools is listed below among the Suggested Readings. It contains many useful tools such as a checklist for recognizing harassment, discussion guides for overcoming myths of masculinity, and various action suggestions. Suggestions for a school campaign to combat violence against women are presented in the White Ribbon Campaign guidelines [28].

These are but a few of the many possibilities for teaching

approaches that can be brought to the task of educating for a culture of peace in a gender perspective. Many more exist and still more can be developed. We suggest possibilities for such development as projects at the end of this section. Others could also be identified and developed by those following this course. What is most important for teachers to recognize is that peace education is a dynamic, developing field which their original contributions can greatly enrich. Should such contributions be cast in a gender perspective, they will provide greater possibilities for the achievement of a culture of peace.

• Foundational Concepts

• Conflict transformation

Conflict transformation is a process of the conversion of a conflict in which those holding divergent and/or opposing goals change their goals and perceptions so as to bring them into accord and complementarity. In so doing, they change themselves and their relationship from adversarial and conflictual to mutual and co-operative. Such a process is referred to as constructive conflict leading to positive change, in which the conflict is transformed through changes in the perceptions, behaviours and values of the conflicting parties.

• Problem-solving

This is a process through which an obstacle to a goal, a potential source of conflict, violence or harm is identified as the subject of an inquiry into modes of overcoming the problem. It involves understanding the various elements of the problem and their causes, and inquiring into possibilities of eliminating or healing the causes and creating alternative situations to the problematic one. Addressing a conflict as a common problem leads to resolution and can initiate transformation.

- **Diagnosis**

Diagnosis is the process of inquiring into the components and causes of a problem, so that it can be fully understood. It is necessary to understand all the complexities of a problem in order to devise a suitable and effective resolution or solution. Gender is often one of the complexities.

- **Prescription**

A prescription is the policy(ies), action or set of actions and changes proposed to heal or eliminate causes of problems and create a new and more positive (peaceful) situation. It is a proposal for a solution or resolution. Most problem-solving and conflict resolution and transformation processes require that a number of alternative prescriptions be considered to determine the course of action that would be most healing and result in the most positive possible outcome, one that is mutually enhancing to all participants.

- **Social action**

Social action comprises non-violent ways in which citizens act together to solve problems and resolve conflicts. It is the most direct route to fulfilling social responsibility and realizing global agency. It is also a means through which citizens learn to be effective social and political actors. Contemporary global civil society is comprised of worldwide networks of social activists.

- # Learning processes and projects

- ## Process

Constructing frameworks of inquiry

Constructing frameworks of inquiry begins with a conceptual identification of that which is to be explored or investigated. Here

Teaching approaches to educating for a culture of peace from a gender perspective

we will posit a problem and a goal around which to construct a problem-solving inquiry. The goal is overcoming sexual harassment in schools so as assure that education can contribute to reducing violence and increasing gender justice. The underlying problematic standing in the way is the sexist socialization children receive from the culture and the gender bias that still prevails in education. The inquiry will be directed towards providing the information and knowledge required to plan a strategy to achieve the goal. We begin with the central query and questions for diagnosis of the problem, then proceed through exploration, to a prescription for solving the problem and assessing the outcomes.

Query: How can we overcome sexual harassment in our schools?
Diagnosis: identifying and defining the problem

1. What is the nature of sexual harassment and how do we recognize it? What values/rights does it violate?

2. What incidents of harassment have occurred in this school; how frequently and under what circumstances?

3. Are these incidents mainly male harassment of female students or vice versa? Is there a climate of gender teasing? Has it become intimidation? Does it involve many or the same few students?

4. What are the 'triggers' of these incidents? What are the deeper causes in the school culture and the wider culture? Which of these causes can the school address? Are some attributable to teaching practices? Does the classroom climate allow for harassment? Does the curriculum reflect sexist biases? Do sports and extracurricular activities contribute to positive or negative gender relations?

Researching the problem: looking for relevant experience and information
(Assuming that this is a co-operative inquiry, this research could be conducted in task groups, reporting to the whole.)

1. Is literature available that relates to the problem as we have diagnosed it? What information and data is most relevant to our situation? Can we find useful information on the Internet?
2. Are there other schools who have dealt with similar problems? What can we learn from their experiences?

Prescription: posing and selecting alternative solutions

1. What relevant insights and information have we gained from our research? How can we apply it to our situation?
2. What are the various possibilities for action to reduce and eliminate sexual harassment in our school? Possibilities for teaching practice, for classroom climate, for the curriculum, for sports and extracurricular activities? (These possibilities could also be identified in task groups.)
3. What effects are each of these possibilities likely to have on students in general, and on boys and girls respectively? What effects on the staff? Which of the action possibilities are most likely to lead to our intended goal? (Assessments of alternatives can be done in task groups, too.)
4. How do we combine these actions into a common plan to resolve the problem of sexual harassment in this school? Do we need to involve others, such as parents, in carrying out this plan?
5. How do we gain the co-operation of the staff and those outside the school who will affect or be affected by this plan? How do we gain the support and co-operation of the students?

Pursuing and assessing the selected solution: acting to affect change

1. How do we begin? What specific steps are to be taken by each staff member?
2. What criteria will we use to assess the effectiveness of the plan? When and at what intervals will we conduct the assessment? How will we determine if, and how, this solution should be revised?

3. What will be the main indicators of success or failure? How can we maintain our commitment to change?

   Note. This framework can be adapted to other inquiries. In planning curricula or research, or any situation in which the pursuit of knowledge or the solution of a problem is sought, from the small specific tasks of learning to overcoming the obstacles to a culture of peace, a plan or a framework to guide the inquiry into the nature of the problem and possibilities to address it will facilitate the task. Well-conducted inquiry yields effective learning, and that can lead to positive change.

• Projects

1. Reflect upon what capacities and skills are required to engage in a process of reconciliation. Make a list of the capacities and the related skills. Form teams to work on the development of a learning procedure to teach one of the skills. Combine the products of the teams into a general curricular plan for teaching reconciliation.
2. Prepare some scenarios of gender conflicts that could occur among the students you will be teaching. Design a process of conflict transformation to deal with such conflicts. Use the design as the basis of a simulation for classroom use.
3. Organize a school campaign to raise awareness about gender violence.

Suggested readings

- **Education and Action Kit,** The White Ribbon Campaign, Men Against Violence Against Women, Toronto, n.d. Available from the campaign at 365 Bloor Street East, Suite 1600, Toronto, Ontario, Canada M4W 3L4. whiterib@idirect.com.
- **Healthy Relationships: A Violence Prevention Curriculum,** Men for Change (in co-operation with the Halifax County–Bedford School District School Board, Nova Scotia) 2nd ed., 1994. Available from Men for Change, Box 3005, Qinpool Postal Outlet, Halifax, Nova Scotia, Canada B3L 4T6. healthy@fox.nstn.ca.

Recommended research

- In order to get a clearer concept of the gender socialization process, conduct a survey among the members of the class and/or other selected sample populations (individual members or teams could select various specific populations.) Pose the following questions to the respondents:
- What are your concepts of the roles and responsibilities of men and women?
- Which of these roles and responsibilities are fixed and unchangeable?
- Which of these roles and responsibilities are flexible and changeable?
- From whom did you learn these roles and responsibilities?
- How did you learn them?
- Look into what others have done to combat sexism and gender bias in education.

Section 9

Creating cultures of peace: the school as an agent of change

Preparatory readings

- **Tolerance – The Threshold of Peace**, Unit 1, Chapter 4, 'Tolerance in the Schools: A Laboratory for the Practice of Peace'.
- **R. W. Connell, Schools' Gender Regimes,** *Teachers College Record* [29].
- **Nonviolence Training Manual,** War Resisters League, 339 Lafayette Street, New York, NY 10012, USA.

• Schools are centres of community

As indicated in Section 2, a culture of peace encompasses all levels and all spheres of human society. There are, however, various institutions that hold special potential and responsibility for inspiring and leading the transformation to a culture of co-operation, peace and human equality. The school, as the agent through which societies prepare their populations for social, cultural and public life, is paramount among these. Yet the school and all of these potential agents of transformation are also immersed in the current culture of competition, war and violence.

The climate of competition and gender inequality that characterizes much contemporary education has already been observed. It must also be observed that schools can be venues of violence. In recent years schools in industrial countries have been the scenes of armed attacks on students and teachers committed by young male students. Many students carry weapons. Male and female students engage in harassment, fighting and vandalism. Some schools still administer corporal punishment, and teachers have been physically threatened by students. Educators in conflict and post-conflict zones struggle to maintain schools in the midst of violence, fear and deprivation. These are only some of the challenges to be faced by schools seeking to educate for peace in the midst of violence. These schools are not zones of peace or realms of truce within embattled societies. They have in many cases become part of the fray. They will require strong, well prepared, committed teachers and the support and encouragement of the communities they serve, if they are to undertake and pursue their roles as agents of transformation to a culture of peace.

Community controversy has also focused on schools and faculties. They have been affected by contention over various community issues, even those that do not directly relate to education. Strongly held religious and political ideologies have been brought into the schools in the form of disputes over curricular content. Controversies have raged over the teaching of values and ethics. The very issues that this unit addresses, peace and gender, have often been the source of contentious public debate over the role of schools in the formation of personal values and social behaviour. Teachers and education authorities who seek to innovate must always have sound rationales and verifiable evidence to uphold arguments in favour of change. There are no areas of education to which this necessity applies more crucially than peace and gender, for these issues touch on the broadest possible range of political, social, cultural and personal concerns.

Involving communities and constituencies from the very beginning of the change process observes fundamental democratic principles, prevents misunderstandings that give rise to controversy and conflict, and helps to assure the community support so vital to any effort to move towards a culture of peace. So, too, the support and co-operation of ministries of education working in the spirit of the Declaration and Integrated Framework of Action on Education for Peace, Human Rights and Democracy can greatly facilitate the process of introducing education for a culture of peace in a gender perspective. Clarity of purpose and the capacity to engage in constructive contention will be significant aids in a process of innovation that might well involve controversy as well as community building.

Schools in virtually all cultures have served as community centres, and at their best are integrated into community life, often taking on tasks other than educating children, such as helping to deal with emergencies and community problems. Teachers and parents are usually members of the same community and their common relationship of care and responsibility for the young is the basis of a productive partnership that could be put in the service of a culture of peace. This partnership could be the vehicle through which ministries of education, school authorities and communities are educated about the needs and possibilities for education for a culture of peace.

If communities are informed about these needs, as well as the sound social and educational rationales that underlie the proposals to fulfil them, and are enlisted in the process of designing and implementing the programmes, they are likely to support the required educational changes. Community members can become allies with educators in their efforts to gain approval and necessary resources from the education authorities. The development of sound school programmes of education for a culture of peace will require co-operative efforts involving teachers, schools, parents, communities and education authorities collaborating on the basis of complementarity of responsibilities and capacities towards a common goal. Such a collaborative effort would, in itself, be a peace education learning experience for all participants. It would bring into play many of the skills that have been designated as basic to functioning as a constructive member of civil society in a culture of peace, especially skills of communication, articulation of new concepts, constructing arguments to support a position, and, very likely, conflict resolution. It would involve all the skills vital to the democratic process and the maintenance of community.

• # Gender issues in schools

Educators have begun to take note of the profound effect of schools
on gender formation and on the relationship of gender identity to
violence in the schools. Their observations echo those noted in Part
One in which feminist peace researchers have, for more than two
decades, demonstrated significant connections between gender
injustice and war. Combined with citizens' concerns about gender
violence, these observations have also led to the development of
curricula such as that described in the previous section. The
current curricular need is to extend these developments as the
concept of conflict processing extends that of conflict resolution to
explore the connections between these gender and violence issues
to the large-scale political violence of war. This study unit seeks to
facilitate an understanding of such connections and to encourage
development of curricula and programmes that will enable teachers
to deal with the problems of violence and gender injustice in their
classrooms and concurrently teach towards a comprehension of
how that learning relates to the global task of eliminating war and
creating a culture of peace. If teachers are to be effective in this vital
task of peace education, they will need the support of gender- and
violence-aware administrators and communities who share the
commitment to gender justice and peace.

Developing gender awareness in schools requires that
teachers and school authorities inquire into gender practices and
behaviours in the schools. It goes deeper than 'formal equality' as
the Australian educator, R. W. Connell, reminds us:

> The educational issues are . . . complex. How real is the formal
> equality provided by coeducation? Are girls benefited in some
> ways, boys in others? How far can we make generalizations about
> 'boys' as a bloc? If boys are having trouble in school, which boys,
> and what are the sources of their trouble? How far can schools
> affect masculinity and its enactment? If they can affect
> masculinity at all, through what kind of programmes, and what
> kind of pedagogy, should they try? [R.W. Connell, Teaching the

Boys: New Research on Masculinity and Gender Strategies for
Schools, *Teachers College Record*, Vol. 98, No. 2, Winter 1996,
p. 207].

Connell, as does this unit, recommends that study of gender
should become a significant component of the curriculum.

> Acquiring knowledge of gender, in one's own society and others,
> is a goal of some importance. Learning the facts of the situation,
> participating in the experiences of other groups, and making a
> critical examination of existing culture and knowledge are general
> educational goals that are quite applicable to this subject matter
> [ibid., p. 221].

This gender and education researcher refers, as well, to the
importance of relationships, just as this unit has advocated
mutually enhancing relationships as integral to peace and gender
justice.

> Two broad types of social relationships are unjust: oppression,
> which restricts the capacity for self-expression; and domination,
> which restricts participation in social decision-making. Both types
> of relationship can be found in schools. The gender practices of
> boys may perpetuate them, and some boys are victims of them.
> Harassment of girls, homophobic abuse, the hierarchy of
> masculinities, bullying, and racial vilification are examples.
> Pursuing justice in schools requires addressing the gender
> patterns that support these practices [ibid., pp. 223–4].

• Classrooms and schools as cultures of peace

Even in the face of the problems posed by the culture of violence
and gender injustice, indeed because of them, educators
throughout the world are taking up the challenge to educate for
peace, and some few of them are doing this so as to incorporate a
gender perspective, argued here to be integral to learning towards a

culture of peace. Schools and the classrooms that comprise them can be organized and conducted so as to be in themselves cultures of peace. By applying to the organization of their tasks the peace purposes and values outlined in this unit, or similar purposes and values derived from their own analysis of and reflection on problems of violence and gender injustice, school authorities can lay the foundations and set the parameters in which teachers can create cultures of peace in their classrooms.

The preliminary reading for this section from *Tolerance* indicates how teachers can assure tolerance in their classrooms. These concepts and approaches to tolerance in schools and classrooms are integral, too, to peaceful and gender-just classrooms. They can be extended to work towards the goals of peace and gender equality just as tolerance is intended to lead to deeper levels of human solidarity and universal respect for the human worth of all cultures, genders and all the ways in which human beings realize affinities and form identities. Teachers can use similar approaches in lessons and learning projects to begin the process of establishing gender tolerance, guiding learners in the development of a community committed to peace, to mutual respect, and to learning how to work towards the realization of such communities in the world outside the classroom.

Multiple variations on co-operative and participatory learning can be applied, such as using ways in which students identify themselves or their preferences to form affinity groups for learning tasks, a variation on previously offered suggestions for co-operative learning and group discussion. Through a process of periodically reformulating these groups around new tasks students could come to know all of their classmates more fully and strengthen the community solidarity of the class. Providing opportunities to perform multiple roles as well as using their particular gifts in learning tasks, especially if these are free of the limitation of gender-role stereotypes, could be a way of helping students to transcend these gender limits. Creative use of the concepts and processes outlined in this unit, adaptations of the learning procedures described in *Tolerance*, and creation of new methods especially designed for a particular learning community or stage in a learning process will enable most teachers to create, at least for a time, such experiences of a culture of peace which would be the most effective learning.

Throughout such attempts, teachers will find the co-operation of their peers an invaluable aid and support. Reviewing learning plans and outcomes with each other, engaging in collaborative curricular design, observing each other's teaching, co-teaching are all modes of co-operative professional learning which can help teachers to become more proficient and to be the kind of communal learners they seek to guide their students to become. To transform schools into the kinds of learning communities that can create cultures of peace, teachers and school administrators need to build solidarity and community among themselves as the foundation of the extended community of the school as a culture of peace.

There are models that offer evidence of the possibilities for change towards positive, gender-just co-operative behaviour that schools can cultivate. Children can be taught not only to respect and co-operate with each other; they can also learn the rewards of such behaviour as they have in the Norwegian UNESCO Associated School where boys have been weaned from competitive, aggressive behaviour by learning that 'It's Fun to Be Nice' (Krokelvdal School, Tromso, Norway; http://www.unesco.org/cpp/wcp). These boys have learned that positive, mutually enhancing relationships with others can be far more satisfying than being 'top man' on the bullying totem pole. Were nations to learn this same lesson, there would be a culture of peace.

Schools and the teachers who staff them can be major actors in devising for their respective nations a globally inspired, culturally relevant learning plan to create a culture of peace. There is much to be learned. The learning possibilities are unlimited. Many have already enlisted in the Global Campaign for Peace Education launched to realize the vision of a culture of peace. We hope that this syllabus will inspire and enable more educators to join in this effort.

• Foundational concepts

• Contention/controversy

Change in a democratic society takes place within a context of
public discussion which often produces a range of opinions and
preferences. Some times factions form, each supporting one
position or proposal over others, or disputing one or more of
them, and controversy ensues. Controversies can strengthen or
weaken communities depending on how they are conducted. If
the contending and disputing arguments are posed in the interest
of determining the best or most effective resolution (rather
than winning arguments as in adversarial debate so prevalent in
the competitive climate of the present global culture, or to
acquire power, the main purpose of most political argument),
the contention is a constructive force which leads to
communal strength and development. Training in constructive
contention is an important area of skill development for a culture
of peace.

• Rationale/argument

A rationale is a set of propositions and arguments to justify or
convince others of the merit of a proposal. Well-documented
arguments and carefully reasoned and constructed rationales are
necessary to the success of proposals for change in a democratic
society, and for providing an adequate basis of assessment of
alternative proposals. Students should have opportunities to
construct clearly reasoned, thoroughly documented arguments.

• Evidence/reasoning

Evidence is the body of fact and documented experience which
attests to the validity and/or merit of a proposal. Evidence is
effective in convincing others of the desirability of a proposal when
it is presented in a sequence of reasoned statements demonstrating

the logic and merit of the proposal. Students should be guided in the practices of gathering, classifying and applying evidence for problem-solving and the contention of public issues.

• Learning processes and projects

• Processes

Constructive/creative contention; social action as education

Constructive and/or creative contention is a variation on the social and learning goal referred to as skills of 'civil disputation' in the assigned readings in *Tolerance*. As defined above constructive contention can lead to the creation of additional, more widely preferred alternatives to contended proposals when the purpose of the discourse is to determine what is best for the community. Constructive/creative contention calls for the exercise of skills of reason and argument, as well as those of clear discussion, reflective listening and participatory hearing emphasized in other sections of this unit. It also depends upon observing the values of respect for others and tolerance of other perspectives or opinions. Conducting a simulation of a constructive contention would be an excellent summary learning process for the conclusion of this unit of study on education for a culture of peace in a gender perspective, for it brings together the fruits of various of the previously suggested learning processes.

1. Start by determining an issue around which there are likely to be some contending opinions, such as, 'Schools should critically examine their roles in gender formation in order to design a programme of change to eliminate gender bias in curriculum and practice, to assure gender equality in all activities, curricular and extra-curricular, and to develop gender-just values and behaviours among the students'; and/or 'Schools should critically examine their roles in supporting the cultural propensity for competition and violence'.

2. Make a statement of rationale for the proposal you adopt as your theme. Include a conceptual definition of its meaning, a description of what it might mean in action, and a diagnostic statement of the problem it seeks to redress.

3. Outline several alternative positions on the theme statement, and assign each position to a team of two or more students. The teams should first review the rationale for the statement, noting points of agreement and disagreement, and/or making restatements of points; next prepare a statement of an alternative to the theme statement or suggest changes in it, containing an alternate diagnosis of the problem if the group does not agree with the original problem description; then prepare a rationale for their theme statement; and finally present suggested approaches to the goal. One team should be prepared to speak on behalf of the original statement. All teams should be gender balanced.

4. Convene a simulated public meeting of the school authority that is empowered to make decisions on the matter of the theme statement. The chairperson informs those in attendance that the purpose of the meeting is not to accept or defeat the action proposed in the theme statement, but to develop a common diagnosis and prescription and come to a communal decision about what should be done about the problem the proposal seeks to redress. Announce the following guidelines for discussion. Make efforts to maintain gender balance throughout the discussion.

Guidelines and procedures

1. All alternative statements of problems and rationales are to be read without comment from the participants. Discussion of each will follow the reading in the same order in which they are read. Remarks concerning the presenters or their previous positions on this or similar issues are not relevant. The discussion will

focus only on the proposals. Civility will be observed in articulating even the most contentious points. Presenters may not be interrupted during the agreed upon speaking time allowed for each. All presenters should be able to count on participatory hearing from all in attendance. Emphasize that this is a communal endeavour.

2. Begin the discussion, taking each proposal in order, beginning with any points of clarification.

3. Try to come to agreement on a statement of the problem, so all can direct their thinking towards a common goal. If necessary, return to a team discussion on this issue to facilitate the process by teams trying to integrate elements of other statements into theirs. If no agreement is reached on the problem, suspend the discussion and set up a task force to determine a commonly acceptable statement of the problem.

4. Once a common problem statement has been devised, open the floor to discussion of the proposal statements and rationales, seeking the aspects of each most relevant to the problem. If there are disagreements on relevance, assess the arguments of the rationales, looking for points of complementarity, commonality as well as aspects that may be incompatible. Remember that the point of contending arguments and positions is not to have one win out over the other, but to come to a problem diagnosis and solution that the community can support as being in its common interest.

5. Rule out the points of incompatibility, and review those that are common and complementary making a summary list. Form another task force to use the list in drafting a new proposal and rationale.

6. Convene a meeting for the presentation of the revised proposal for achieving the purpose of responding to the initial problem statement and arrange a planning group to design a plan for implementation. If the implementation proposal requires a

Creating cultures of peace: the school as an agent of change

constructive contention process, set one up. If the revised proposal also calls for continued discussion to reach consensus, continue the constructive contention process through more rounds until consensus is reached.

7. Throughout the process, the facilitators should work to maintain civility and communality in the discussions. Any breaches should be acknowledged and reconciled.

• **Projects**

Form student teams to practise teaching lessons on peace and gender justice, each member taking a turn at teaching and receiving suggestions for improvement of the content and presentation of the lesson.

Form task groups of class members to plan a collaborative initiative in which schools, parents and community prepare and present a proposal for implementing and funding, if necessary, peace education in the community's schools. Each group should take one constituency of the community and assess what concerns they might have about education for a culture of peace in a gender perspective, planning ways in which to meet those concerns. Then all groups could make a general plan involving all constituencies and prepare an agenda for a community meeting to call for the introduction of education for a culture of peace into the schools.

Suggested readings

- **Steven Walker and Len Barton** (eds.), *Gender, Class and Education*, Barcombe, Lewes, Falmer, 1983.
- **Gordon Fellman**, *Rambo and the Dalai Lama: The Compulsion to Win and its threat to Human Survival*, Albany, State University of New York Press, 1998.
- **Linda Lantieri**, *Waging Peace in Our Schools*, Boston, Beacon Press, 1996.

Recommended research

- Inquire into the possibility that violence occurs in the schools of your community. If you uncover any incidents of violence, inquire further to determine some of the contributing factors. Be sure to include cultural influences, the socialization process, peer pressure, gender factors and adult responsibility. Once you have reviewed and assessed your findings, plan a programme in which the schools might educate to overcome such instances and contribute to a more peaceful climate in your community.

- Develop a research project for students on violence and gender bias in youth culture. Be sure to include inquiry into lyrics of popular music, videos, television, advertising, youth values and activities. Involve the media.

- Develop a violence-awareness instrument to use as an instructional device. The instrument should assess student awareness of: (a) organized violence, including gang violence and other forms of warfare; (b) physical violence including various kinds of gender and child abuse, rape, enforced prostitution; (c) social violence, including crime, sexual and racial discrimination; (d) structural/economic violence including exploitation of labour, unfair trade practices, price gouging in poor areas; (e) cultural violence, including aspects of the traditional (culture-specific customs and practices), classical and popular culture.

Supplementary materials

Most of the supplemental materials that have been suggested throughout the text are available on the World Wide Web, or from UNESCO Publishing [http://upo.unesco.org]. They are listed below with the websites on which they may be found. Instructors may find it helpful to download them and place hard copies in the library for student use. Those materials not posted on other sites are to be posted on the site of the UNESCO Women and a Culture of Peace Programme, which is periodically updated and augmented:
[http://www.unesco.org/cpp/wcp].

1. Declaration and Integrated Framework of Action on Education for Peace, Human Rights and Democracy.
   URL: http://www.unesco.org/education/nfsunesco/pdf/REV_74_E.PDF
2. Universal Declaration of Human Rights.
   URL: http://www.unhchr.ch/udhr/index.htm
3. Convention on the Elimination of All Forms of Discrimination against Women (CEDAW).
   URL: http://www.unhchr.ch/html/menu3/b/e1cedaw.htm
4. Declaration and Programme of Action of the Decade for Culture of Peace and Nonviolence for the Children of the World.
   URL: http://www.unesco.org/cpp/uk/declarations/2000.htm
5. UNESCO, Statement on Women's Contribution to a Culture of Peace. Fourth World Conference on Women, Beijing, China, 4–15 September 1995.
   URL: http://www.unesco.org/cpp/uk/declarations/wcpbei.htm
6. International Commission on Education for the Twenty-first Century. *Learning: The Treasure Within*. Paris, UNESCO Publishing, 1996.

7. Seville Statement on Violence.
URL: http://www.unesco.org/cpp/uk/declarations/seville.pdf

8. Excerpts from Jack Fraenkel, Margaret Carter and Betty A. Reardon,
(eds.), *Peacekeeping*.
URL: http://www.haguepeace.org (click on Global Campaign for
Peace Education)

9. Guidelines for a Gender Perspective and Indicators of Gender
Tolerance.
URL: http://www.haguepeace.org (click on Global Campaign for
Peace Education)

10. UNESCO Manifesto 2000 for a Culture of Peace and Non-violence.
URL: http://www3.unesco.org/manifesto2000/

11. The Hague Agenda for the 21st Century.
URL: http://www.haguepeace.org/

12. *Global Citizenship: A Draft Declaration*, October 1999.
URL: http://www.haguepeace.org (click on Global Campaign for
Peace Education)

13. Betty A. Reardon, Excellence in Education through Peacemaking,
The Journal of Global Education, Breakthrough, Spring/Summer 1987 :
(rpt. of Ch. 7, in B. A. Reardon, *Comprehensive Peace Education*,
pp. 616, N.Y., Teachers College Press, 1988 [out print]).
URL: http://www.haguepeace.org (click on Global Campaign for
Peace Education)

14. Beijing Platform for Action.
URL: http://www.un.org/womenwatch/daw/beijing/platform/

15. Bibliography on the Theory and Practice of Peace Education.
URL: http://www.haguepeace.org (click on Global Campaign for
Peace Education)

16. *World Declaration on Education for All: Meeting Basic Learning Needs* and
Framework for Action: Meeting Basic Learning Needs (World
Conference on Education for All, Jomtien, Thailand, 5–9 March
1990).
URL: http://www.unesco.org/education/efa/ed_for_all/background/
background_documents.shtml

17. *The Dakar Framework for Action – Education for All: Meeting our
Collective Commitments* (World Education Forum, Dakar, Senegal,
26–28 April 2000).
URL: http://www.unesco.org/education/efa/wef_2000/index.shtml

18. Bibliography on Women and Peace Issues.
URL: http://www.peacewomen.org

19. Declaration on the Elimination of all Forms of Violence against Women.
    URL: http://www.unhchr.ch/html/menu3/b/21.htm
20. Optional Protocol to CEDAW.
    URL: http://www.unhchr.ch/html/menu3/b/opt_cedaw.htm
21. *A Declaration of Human Rights in a Gender Perspective.*
    URL: http://www.pdhre.org
22. *Universal Declaration of Human Responsibilities*, drafted by Hans Kung
    for the Inter-Action Council.
23. Final Documents of the Zanzibar Conference, Paris, UNESCO, 1999.
    URL: http://www.unesco.org/cpp/uk/declarations/zanzibar.htm
24. Windhoek Declaration.
    URL: http://www.unifem.undp.org/unseccouncil/windhoek.html
25. How to Deal with Anger, from the site *Healthy Relationships, Violence
    Prevention Curriculum*, Halifax, Canada, Men For Change.
    URL: http://fox.nstn.ca/~healthy
26. FAWE, *Promoting Women's Participation in Conflict Resolution to Build a
    Culture of Peace*, UNESCO (forthcoming).
27. *Conflict Processing Framework.*
    URL: http://www.haguepeace.org (click on Global Campaign for
    Peace Education)
28. White Ribbon, Education and Action Kit, guidelines for a school
    campaign to combat violence against women.
    URL: http://www.whiteribbon.ca
29. Robert Connell, *Schools' Gender Regimes, Teachers College Record.*
    Inquiries should be sent to Teachers College #103, Columbia
    University, New York, N. Y. 10027, United States of America.
30. WINGHS (Women's International Network for Gender and Security).
    Statement and Questions.
    URL: http://www.haguepeace.org (click on Global Campaign for
    Peace Education)
31. Convention on the Rights of the Child.
    URL: http://www.unhchr.ch/html/menu3/b/k2crc.htm
32. Hanoi Declaration and Asian Women's Plan of Action for a Culture of
    Peace and Sustainable Development.
    URL: http://www.unesco.org/cpp/uk/projects/wcpviet.htm